taste of home.
light COOKING
DONE RIGHT

45

taste of home

light COOKING
DONE RIGHT

Senior Vice President, Editor in Chief	Catherine Cassidy
Vice President, Executive Editor/Books	Heidi Reuter Lloyd
Creative Director	Ardyth Cope
Food Director	Diane Werner RD
Senior Editor/Books	Mark Hagen
Editors	Amy Glander, Peggy Woodward RD
Art Director	Rudy Krochalk
Content Production Supervisor	Julie Wagner
Layout Designer	Kathleen Bump
Proofreader	Linne Bruskewitz
Recipe Asset Management System	Coleen Martin, Sue A. Jurack
Premedia Supervisor	Scott Berger
Recipe Testing and Editing	Taste of Home Test Kitchen
Food Photography	Taste of Home Photo Studio
Editorial Assistant	Barb Czysz
Cover Photo Photographer	Rob Hagen
Cover Photo Set Stylist	Melissa Haberman
Cover Photo Food Stylist	Kaitlyn Besasie

Chief Marketing Officer	Lisa Karpinski
Vice President/Book Marketing	Dan Fink

The Reader's Digest Association, Inc.

President and Chief Executive Officer	Mary G. Berner
President, U.S. Affinities	Suzanne M. Grimes
SVP, Chief Marketing Officer	Amy J. Radin
President, Global Consumer Marketing	Dawn M. Zier

Pictured on front cover: Turkey Tomato Pizza (p. 69)
Pictured on back cover: Roasted Potato Salad (p. 43), Green 'n' Gold Egg Bake (p. 17),
Double Chocolate Cupcakes (p. 96)

International Standard Book Number (10): 0-89821-759-8
International Standard Book Number (13): 978-0-89821-759-9
Library of Congress Control Number: 2009931201

Timeless Recipes from Trusted Home Cooks® is a registered trademark of Reiman Media Group, Inc.
For other Taste of Home books and products, visit ShopTasteofHome.com.

Printed in China.
3 5 7 9 10 8 6 4 2

Taste of Home is a registered trademark of The Reader's Digest Association, Inc.

table of contents

100

Light Cooking Done Right makes a great gift for anyone who wants to whip up good-for-you fare that tastes delicious. To order additional copies, specify item number 39461 and send $14.99 (plus $4.99 shipping/processing for one book, $5.99 for two or more) to: Shop Taste of Home, Suite 1115, P.O. Box 26820, Lehigh Valley, PA 18002-6280. To order by credit card, call toll-free 1-800/880-3012.

discover 207 deliciously light recipes!

All good home cooks have been faced with the conundrum of creating nutritionally balanced meals that don't fall short on the flavors their families love. Now it's easier than ever to whip up delicious, good-for-you fare that requires little fuss and is guaranteed to please! *Light Cooking Done Right* brings more than 200 mouth-watering recipes to the table that are as healthful as they are delectable.

No matter what time of day, a wholesome meal is at your fingertips. Start your morning off right with a breakfast delight such as Green 'n' Gold Egg Bake (p. 17). For a nutritious lunch, enjoy garden-fresh Orange Cucumber Tossed Salad (p. 49) with a cup of simmering Roasted Chicken Noodle Soup (p. 45). When it's time to ring the dinner bell, take a big bite into cheesy Turkey Tomato Pizza (p. 69). After eating a health-smart dinner it's okay to indulge in a slimmed-down dessert like luscious Light Lemon Cheesecake (p. 93).

These recipes and more come complete with Nutrition Facts, Diabetic Exchanges and handy icons to guide you, so it's a cinch to select family-pleasing recipes for any day of the week. You'll also find helpful dietary information, learn the value of nutrient-rich foods and discover simple strategies to monitor portion size and opt for lighter ingredients over their higher-calorie counterparts.

Turn to any one of the delicious, healthful, hassle-free wonders on the pages that follow, and feel good knowing you're feeding your family the very best. Every recipe has been tested by our home economists and reviewed by our team of Registered Dietitians, so you're guaranteed nutritious and reliable results every time. With *Light Cooking Done Right*, eating healthy has never been so easy...or tasted so great!

helpful health categories

Use these four at-a-glance icons to help you identify dishes best suited to your own nutritional needs.

(LF) LOW-FAT — one serving contains 3 grams or less of fat

(LS) LOW-SODIUM — one serving contains 140 milligrams or less of sodium

(LC) LOW-CARBOHYDRATE — one serving contains 15 grams or less of carbohydrates

(ML) MEATLESS — any dish that contains no meat

complete nutrition facts

All recipes in this book fit into a balanced diet for healthy adults. Every recipe also includes complete Nutrition Facts, calculated with these guidelines:

- When a choice of ingredients is given in a recipe (such as 1/3 cup of sour cream *or* plain yogurt), the first ingredient listed is always the one calculated in the Nutrition Facts.

- When a range is given for an ingredient (such as 2 to 3 teaspoons), we calculate the first amount given.

- Only the amount of marinade absorbed during preparation is calculated.

- Garnishes listed in a recipe are typically included in calculations.

The Diabetic Exchanges are in accordance with the guidelines from the American Diabetic and American Dietetic Associations. All the recipes in this book are suitable for diabetics.

use these simple strategies
for eating healthy and living well

EAT FOR GOOD HEALTH

A healthful lifestyle is all about balance, and making smart food choices is the first step. According to USDA guidelines, a smart diet is one that emphasizes vegetables, fruits, whole grains and low-fat or fat-free milk products. It also includes lean meats, poultry, fish, beans, eggs, nuts and other protein-packed foods. Finally, a healthful diet is low in saturated fat, trans fat, cholesterol, sodium and added sugars.

Strive for variety in your daily meals, and you'll see how easy it is to hit your nutrition goals. Consider the following points when selecting foods, and visit www.MyPyramid.gov for more detailed dietary information from the USDA.

KNOW THE VALUE OF VEGGIES

Vegetables are as close to the perfect food as there is. And the more you eat, the better because these wonder foods are filled with health-enhancing vitamins, minerals and phytochemicals, which may help lower the risk of type 2 diabetes and cancer, lower blood pressure and drop levels of LDL (bad) cholesterol. Include plenty of colorful options such as broccoli, carrots, cauliflower and beans, and eat plenty of dark green leafy foods like spinach, kale or leaf lettuces. The USDA recommends consuming at least 2 to 3 cups—or three to five servings—of vegetables every day, depending on your calorie needs.

HAVE A FRUIT-A-LICIOUS DAY

Fruit provides essential vitamins, minerals, fiber and antioxidants, which may help ward off heart disease, cancer and other health maladies. Eat a variety of fresh, frozen, canned, dried and 100% fruit juices. Try to consume at least 1-1/2 to 2 cups of fruit, or two to four servings, per day.

MAKE HALF YOUR GRAINS WHOLE

Look to whole grains as your primary source of grains. Cut back on refined grains such as white bread, white rice or many ready-to-eat cereals like corn flakes. The USDA recommends at least half of all the grains consumed be whole. You can stock up on these by eating whole grain breads, brown rice, oatmeal and whole wheat pastas. Whole grains help boost your intake of fiber, which can help decrease cholesterol and improve digestion. Aim for about 25 to 30 grams of fiber per day.

GO CRAZY FOR CALCIUM

For stronger bones, consume about three servings of calcium-rich foods, such as milk, yogurt and cheese each day. Reach for the low- or fat-free varieties and go easy on whole milk and full-fat dairy products. These foods are not only rich in calcium, but also vitamin D and protein. If you're vegan, lactose-intolerant or simply don't like dairy products, select nondairy foods that are high in calcium, such as tofu, spinach or broccoli, or calcium-fortified foods such as soy milk or orange juice. Make it a goal to get about 1,000 to 1,200 mg of calcium each day.

GET LEAN WITH PROTEIN

Bake, broil or grill lean meats and poultry, and add more fish, seafood, beans, peas, nuts and seeds to your meal plan. Protein-packed foods will provide you with the essential amino acids, minerals and vitamins necessary for energy and building muscle. Aim for about 50 grams of protein per day.

KNOW YOUR FATS

Choose foods low in saturated fat, preferably no more than 10% of your total daily calories. Choose oils that are high in mono- and polyunsaturated fat like olive, canola, corn, soybean or safflower oils. Limit or avoid solid fats such as butter, shortening and lard, and foods that contain these. Aim for zero trans fat—a big culprit in commercial and restaurant foods.

WATCH YOUR PORTIONS

Living in a world of super-sized fare, it's easy to forget that the amount of food you eat is just as important as the types of foods you choose.

Pay attention to the serving size listed on Nutrition Facts labels and take note of how many servings you're actually eating of a particular food. Your first inclination might be to scoop up a spoonful, which could be twice the actual serving size. Try these tips to better control serving sizes:

- Ask for a to-go container at restaurants and pack food to take home before you begin eating.

- Avoid serving meals "family style." Portion food onto smaller dinner plates and bring it to the table, keeping seconds out of sight.

- Don't eat directly from bags or cartons. Set the food on a plate or napkin and put the rest away.

- Use visual cues. A reasonable serving of meat should be the size of a deck of cards, a piece of fruit the size of your fist, a piece of cheese the size of your thumb and a serving of pasta or rice should be the size of a tennis ball.

EXERCISE

Physical activity is a cornerstone of total wellness because it helps manage body weight, improves fitness and lowers the risk of heart disease, type 2 diabetes and high blood pressure. Before starting an exercise program, consult your doctor for recommendations tailored to your level of fitness and appropriate for your health. For better results, work toward these goals:

- Adults should be physically active for at least 30 minutes most days of the week. Children and teens should be physically active for 60 minutes almost every day.

- Keep your workouts exciting by varying your exercises, listening to music to get you pumped up or working out with a friend to help keep you accountable.

- Slowly increase the level of intensity and the amount of time you are physically active. This will reap even greater health benefits in addition to building stronger muscles and controlling body weight. About 60 minutes of high-intensity physical exercise may be needed to prevent weight gain and 60-90 minutes to sustain weight loss.

74   53   102

take the first step!

Now that you're armed with essential nutritional information and a big selection of light-done-right recipes, you are ready to begin a brand-new lifestyle and indulge in nutritious meals the whole family will love! Use the recipes on the pages that follow as inspiration for a lifetime of good health.

breakfast & brunch

brunch pizza squares page 13

orange oatmeal

orange oatmeal LF ML

*This oatmeal is great for breakfast because it's quick yet out of the ordinary. The
orange juice adds a burst of flavor and lots of vitamin C, too.*

—Bernice Haack, Milwaukee, Wisconsin

1	cup water	1/4	teaspoon grated orange peel
3/4	cup orange juice	1	to 2 tablespoons brown sugar
1/8	teaspoon salt		
1	cup quick-cooking oats		

In a small saucepan, bring the water, orange juice and salt to a boil. Stir in oats
and cook for 1 minute or until oatmeal reaches desired consistency. Stir in orange peel. Serve with brown sugar. **YIELD: 2 SERVINGS.**

NUTRITION FACTS: 1 serving (prepared with 1 tablespoon brown sugar) equals 222 calories,
3 g fat (trace saturated fat), 0 cholesterol, 151 mg sodium, 43 g carbohydrate, 4 g fiber, 7 g protein. **DIABETIC EXCHANGES:** 2 starch, 1 fruit.

Light
COOKING TIP

*Oatmeal contains
soluble fiber, which helps
reduce your low-density
lipoprotein (LDL) or
"bad" cholesterol.
Soluble fiber also helps
you feel fuller longer so
it's great for morning
meals. Add fruit, such as
bananas or apples, to
add even more fiber.*

makeover sausage pinwheels with herb gravy

This lighter version of a classic recipe tastes just as delicious as the original, but without all the fat and calories.
—*Taste of Home Test Kitchen*

2-1/4	cups all-purpose flour, *divided*
2	teaspoons baking powder
1-1/4	teaspoons minced chives, *divided*
1-1/4	teaspoons dried parsley flakes, *divided*
3/4	teaspoon dried tarragon, *divided*
1/2	teaspoon seasoned salt
1/2	teaspoon sugar
1/4	teaspoon baking soda
2	tablespoons plus 2 teaspoons cold butter, *divided*
3/4	cup buttermilk
12	ounces reduced-fat bulk pork sausage
2	cups fat-free half-and-half
2	teaspoons chicken bouillon granules
1/4	teaspoon pepper

Dash crushed red pepper flakes

In a large bowl, combine 2 cups flour, the baking powder, 3/4 teaspoon chives, 3/4 teaspoon parsley, 1/2 teaspoon tarragon, seasoned salt, sugar and baking soda. Cut in 2 tablespoons butter until mixture resembles coarse crumbs. Stir in buttermilk. On a floured surface, roll or pat dough into a 14-in. x 10-in. rectangle.

Between two sheets of waxed paper, roll or pat sausage into a 14-in. x 8-in. rectangle. Peel off one side of waxed paper. Place sausage side on top of dough. Peel off remaining waxed paper. Starting with the long side covered with sausage, roll up jelly-roll style; pinch seam to seal. Wrap in waxed paper. Refrigerate for 45 minutes.

Remove waxed paper; cut roll into 1-in. slices. Place cut side down in a 13-in. x 9-in. baking pan coated with cooking spray. Bake at 400° for 30-35 minutes or until golden brown.

For gravy, place remaining flour in a saucepan. Gradually stir in the half-and-half, bouillon, pepper, pepper flakes and remaining chives, parsley and tarragon until smooth. Bring to a boil over medium-low heat; cook and stir for 1-2 minutes or until thickened. remove from the heat; stir in remaining butter. Serve immediately with pinwheels. **YIELD: 7 SERVINGS.**

NUTRITION FACTS: 2 pinwheels with 1/4 cup gravy equals 363 calories, 14 g fat (6 g saturated fat), 13 mg cholesterol, 999 mg sodium, 40 g carbohydrate, 1 g fiber, 16 g protein. **DIABETIC EXCHANGES:** 2 starch, 2 fat, 1 lean meat, 1/2 fat-free milk.

makeover sausage pinwheels with herb gravy

do-ahead brunch bake

I wake up my clan with this convenient early-morning casserole that I assemble the night before. It features low-fat ingredients but is still hearty enough to keep them satisfied.
—*Joy Maynard, St. Ignatius, Montana*

8	frozen hash brown patties
1	package (8 ounces) thinly sliced fully cooked ham, chopped
1-1/4	cups shredded reduced-fat cheddar cheese, *divided*
2	cups fat-free milk
1	can (10-3/4 ounces) reduced-fat reduced-sodium condensed cream of mushroom soup, undiluted
1	cup egg substitute
1	teaspoon ground mustard
1/4	teaspoon pepper

Place the potato patties in a 13-in. x 9-in. baking dish coated with cooking spray. Top with ham and 1 cup cheese. Combine milk, soup, egg substitute, mustard and pepper; pour over cheese. Cover and refrigerate overnight.

Remove from the refrigerator 30 minutes before baking. Bake at 350° for 1 hour. Uncover and sprinkle with the remaining cheese. Bake 20-25 minutes longer or until a knife inserted near the center comes out clean. Let stand 10 minutes before serving. **YIELD: 12 SERVINGS.**

NUTRITION FACTS: 1 serving equals 122 calories, 5 g fat (0 saturated fat), 13 mg cholesterol, 463 mg sodium, 9 g carbohydrate, trace fiber, 11 g protein. **DIABETIC EXCHANGES:** 1 meat, 1/2 starch.

cherry almond granola

minutes or until golden brown, stirring occasionally. Cool completely. Serve with yogurt if desired. Store in an airtight container. **YIELD: 3 QUARTS.**

NUTRITION FACTS: 1/2 cup granola equals 222 calories, 5 g fat (1 g saturated fat), trace cholesterol, 15 mg sodium, 38 g carbohydrate, 3 g fiber, 5 g protein. **DIABETIC EXCHANGES:** 1-1/2 fruit, 1 starch, 1 fat.

breakfast pizza Ⓛ

This breakfast pizza is a great way to get all the satisfaction of a hearty breakfast dish without consuming an entire day's worth of calories in one sitting. If you like, add a variety of veggies to pack in extra nutrients.

—June Robinson, Bastrop, Louisiana

    1   tube (8 ounces) refrigerated reduced-fat crescent rolls
    1   pound bulk turkey sausage
  3/4   cup egg substitute
  1/3   cup fat-free milk
  3/4   teaspoon dried oregano
  1/2   teaspoon pepper
    2   cups (8 ounces) shredded fat-free pizza cheese

Separate crescent dough into eight triangles and place on a greased 12-in. round pizza pan with points toward the center. Press onto bottom and up sides of pan to form a crust; seal perforations. Bake at 375° for 8 minutes.

Meanwhile, in a large skillet, brown sausage until no longer pink; drain. Sprinkle over crust.

In a small bowl, combine the egg substitute, milk, oregano and pepper. Carefully pour over the sausage. Reduce heat to 350° and bake for 25 minutes. Top with cheese; bake 5 minutes longer. **YIELD: 8 SERVINGS.**

NUTRITION FACTS: 1 piece equals 239 calories, 10 g fat (0 saturated fat), 39 mg cholesterol, 756 mg sodium, 14 g carbohydrate, 0 fiber, 21 g protein. **DIABETIC EXCHANGES:** 2-1/2 lean meat, 1 starch, 1/2 fat.

cherry almond granola Ⓛ Ⓜ

Skim milk turns this crunchy snack into a healthful breakfast cereal, while a dollop of low-fat yogurt makes it a delectable dessert. Try adding a little baking cocoa to the brown sugar for a chocolaty flavor twist.

—Deborah Purdue, Freeland, Michigan

    1   cup packed brown sugar
  1/2   cup nonfat dry milk powder
  1/2   cup honey
  1/3   cup unsweetened apple juice concentrate
    2   tablespoons canola oil
    3   teaspoons almond extract
    6   cups old-fashioned oats
1-1/2   cups dried cherries *or* cranberries
    1   cup slivered almonds
Fat-free vanilla yogurt, optional

In a large saucepan, combine the brown sugar, milk powder, honey, apple juice concentrate and oil. Cook and stir over medium heat until sugar is dissolved; stir in extract. In a large bowl, combine the oats, cherries and almonds. Drizzle with sugar mixture and mix well.

Spread in a thin layer in two 15-in. x 10-in. x 1-in. baking pans coated with cooking spray. Bake at 375° for 15-20

Light COOKING TIP

Buy sausage in large quantities when it's on sale. Brown it, then pack it in small resealable plastic bags. Date the bags and pop them in the freezer. You'll have browned sausage readily available to perk up a quick omelet or breakfast pizza.

ham and corn souffle

ham and corn souffle

Breakfast is bound to be the most memorable meal of the day with this attractive souffle as its focus. The ham and corn enhance the cheesy egg flavor, and the casserole's texture is moist and light. A puffed golden top makes it look too pretty to eat...but nobody can resist!
—Margaret Haugh Heilman, Houston, Texas

4	egg whites
2	teaspoons dry bread crumbs
1-1/2	cups frozen corn, thawed
2	green onions, thinly sliced
2/3	cup diced fully cooked lean ham
1/4	cup all-purpose flour
1/4	teaspoon salt
1/8	teaspoon cayenne pepper
1	cup fat-free milk
1/2	cup shredded reduced-fat sharp cheddar cheese
2	egg yolks
1/2	teaspoon cream of tartar

Place egg whites in a large bowl; let stand at room temperature for 30 minutes. Coat a 1-1/2-qt. baking dish with cooking spray and lightly sprinkle with bread crumbs; set aside.

In a large nonstick skillet coated with cooking spray, cook corn and onions until tender. Remove from the heat; stir in ham and set aside.

In a small saucepan, combine the flour, salt and cayenne; gradually whisk in milk until smooth. Bring to a boil; cook and stir for 2 minutes or until thickened. Remove from the heat; stir in cheese until melted. Transfer to a large bowl; stir in corn mixture. Stir a small amount of hot mixture into egg yolks; return all to the bowl, stirring constantly. Cool slightly.

Add cream of tartar to egg whites; beat until stiff peaks form. With a spatula, fold a fourth of the egg whites into the milk mixture until no white streaks remain. Fold in remaining egg whites until combined.

Transfer to prepared dish. Bake at 325° for 50-55 minutes or until top is puffed and center appears set. Serve immediately. **YIELD: 4 SERVINGS.**

NUTRITION FACTS: 1 serving equals 248 calories, 7 g fat (3 g saturated fat), 123 mg cholesterol, 577 mg sodium, 28 g carbohydrate, 2 g fiber, 20 g protein. **DIABETIC EXCHANGES:** 2 starch, 2 lean meat.

pecan waffles Ⓜ

Serve these wonderful waffles on your morning menu, and you'll have no trouble calling your brood to the table!
—Susan Bell, Spruce Pine, North Carolina

1-1/4	cups all-purpose flour
1/4	cup wheat bran
1	tablespoon sugar
2-1/2	teaspoons baking powder
1/2	teaspoon salt
1	egg
1	egg white
1-1/2	cups fat-free milk
2	tablespoons canola oil
1/3	cup chopped pecans

In a large bowl, combine the flour, bran, sugar, baking powder and salt. In another bowl, combine the egg, egg white, milk and oil; add to the dry ingredients. Fold in pecans.

Bake in a preheated waffle iron according to manufacturer's directions until waffles are golden brown. **YIELD: 6 WAFFLES (6-1/2-INCH DIAMETER).**

NUTRITION FACTS: 1 waffle equals 233 calories, 11 g fat (1 g saturated fat), 37 mg cholesterol, 344 mg sodium, 28 g carbohydrate, 2 g fiber, 8 g protein. **DIABETIC EXCHANGES:** 2 starch, 2 fat.

pecan waffles

veggie cheese omelet (LC) (ML)

Here's the the perfect single serving for breakfast. The recipe is a great way to use zucchini from the garden.
—Jan Collier, Lubbock, Texas

1/4 cup egg substitute
2 tablespoons shredded Parmesan cheese, *divided*
1/8 teaspoon dried oregano
Dash garlic powder and pepper
1/4 cup sliced zucchini
2 tablespoons diced sweet red pepper
1 bacon strip, cooked and crumbled
1/3 cup shredded cheddar cheese

In a small bowl, combine the egg substitute, 1 tablespoon Parmesan cheese and seasonings. Coat an 8-in. nonstick skillet with cooking spray and place over medium heat. Pour egg mixture into skillet.

As egg sets, lift edges, letting uncooked portion flow underneath. When the eggs are set, layer the zucchini, red pepper, bacon and cheddar cheese on one side; fold omelet in half. Sprinkle top with remaining Parmesan cheese. Remove from the heat; cover and let stand for 3-4 minutes or until cheese is melted. YIELD: 1 SERVING.

NUTRITION FACTS: 1 serving equals 229 calories, 14 g fat, (8 g saturated fat), 40 mg cholesterol, 414 mg sodium, 5 g carbohydrate, 1 g fiber, 22 g protein. DIABETIC EXCHANGES: 3 lean meat, 1 vegetable, 1 fat.

orange whole wheat pancakes (LF) (ML)

Friends and family will flip over these light whole wheat pancakes featuring a sunny twist of citrus. Feel free to mix in raisins or dried cranberries to add a bit of chewy sweetness.
—Earl Brunner, Las Vegas, Nevada

3 egg whites
1 cup orange juice
1/3 cup unsweetened applesauce
1/4 teaspoon orange extract
1-1/4 cups whole wheat flour
2 tablespoons sugar
2 teaspoons baking powder
1/2 teaspoon salt
1/2 cup orange marmalade

In a blender, combine the first four ingredients. Cover and process until smooth. In a large bowl, combine the flour, sugar, baking powder and salt; make a well. Add orange juice mixture; stir just until moistened.

Pour batter by 2 tablespoonfuls onto a hot griddle coated with cooking spray. Turn when bubbles form on top of pancake; cook until second side is golden brown. Serve with marmalade. YIELD: 16 PANCAKES.

NUTRITION FACTS: 2 pancakes equals 150 calories, trace fat (trace saturated fat), 0 cholesterol, 238 mg sodium, 35 g carbohydrate, 3 g fiber, 4 g protein. DIABETIC EXCHANGES: 1-1/2 starch, 1/2 fruit.

brunch pizza squares

brunch pizza squares (LC)

Guests always ask me for the recipe for these delectable pizza squares. Refrigerated cresent rolls and precooked sausage from my freezer keep preparation easy. Feel free to use turkey sausage, egg substitute and other reduced-fat ingredients for a lighter version of this dish.
—LaChelle Olivet, Pace, Florida

1 pound bulk pork sausage
1 tube (8 ounces) refrigerated crescent rolls
4 eggs
2 tablespoons milk
1/8 teaspoon pepper
3/4 cup shredded cheddar cheese

In a large skillet, crumble sausage and cook over medium heat until no longer pink; drain. Unroll crescent dough onto the bottom and 1/2 in. up the sides of a lightly greased 13-in. x 9-in. baking pan; seal seams. Sprinkle with sausage.

In a large bowl, beat the eggs, milk and pepper; pour over sausage. Sprinkle with cheese.

Bake, uncovered, at 400° for 15 minutes or until a knife inserted in the center comes out clean. YIELD: 8 SERVINGS.

NUTRITION FACTS: 1 serving (prepared with turkey sausage, egg substitute equivalent to 4 eggs, fat-free milk and reduced-fat crescent rolls and cheese) equals 243 calories, 13 g fat (0 saturated fat), 50 mg cholesterol, 687 mg sodium, 14 g carbohydrate, 1 g fiber, 18 g protein. DIABETIC EXCHANGES: 2 meat, 1 starch, 1/2 fat.

fruity oatmeal

I never liked oatmeal until my mom found this wonderful combination of uncooked oats and fresh fruit. Now I often make it myself for breakfast or an after-school snack.
—*Sarah Hunt, Everett, Washington*

- 1/3 cup old-fashioned oats
- 1 teaspoon oat bran
- 1/3 cup diced unpeeled tart apple
- 1 medium firm banana, diced
- 1/4 cup halved seedless grapes
- 2 tablespoons raisins
- 1 tablespoon sliced almonds

Milk *or* yogurt, optional

In a large bowl, toss the first seven ingredients; divide between two small bowls. Serve with milk or yogurt if desired. **YIELD: 2 SERVINGS.**

NUTRITION FACTS: 1/2-cup serving (calculated without milk and yogurt) equals 182 calories, 4 g fat (0 saturated fat), 0 cholesterol, 5 mg sodium, 37 g carbohydrate, 0 fiber, 4 g protein. **DIABETIC EXCHANGES:** 1-1/2 fruit, 1 starch, 1/2 fat.

fruity oatmeal

confetti scrambled egg pockets

This sunny specialty is a colorful crowd-pleaser. My eight grandchildren often enjoy these egg-packed pitas for Saturday morning brunch...or with a light salad for supper.
—*Dixie Terry, Goreville, Illinois*

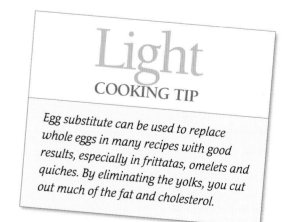

confetti scrambled egg pockets

- 1 cup fresh *or* frozen corn
- 1/4 cup chopped green pepper
- 2 tablespoons chopped onion
- 1 jar (2 ounces) diced pimientos, drained
- 1 tablespoon butter
- 1-1/4 cups egg substitute
- 3 eggs
- 1/4 cup fat-free evaporated milk
- 1/2 teaspoon seasoned salt
- 1 medium tomato, seeded and chopped
- 1 green onion, sliced
- 3 whole wheat pita breads (6 inches), halved

In a large nonstick skillet, saute the corn, green pepper, onion and the pimientos in butter for 5-7 minutes or until tender.

In a large bowl, combine the egg substitute, eggs, milk and salt; pour into skillet. Cook and stir over medium heat until eggs are completely set. Stir in the tomato and green onion. Spoon about 2/3 cup into each pita half. **YIELD: 6 SERVINGS.**

NUTRITION FACTS: 1 filled pita half equals 207 calories, 6 g fat (2 g saturated fat), 112 mg cholesterol, 538 mg sodium, 28 g carbohydrate, 4 g fiber, 13 g protein. **DIABETIC EXCHANGES:** 1-1/2 starch, 1 lean meat, 1 vegetable, 1/2 fat.

Light
COOKING TIP

Egg substitute can be used to replace whole eggs in many recipes with good results, especially in frittatas, omelets and quiches. By eliminating the yolks, you cut out much of the fat and cholesterol.

six-veggie bake (LF) (ML)

I altered the original recipe for this strata-like dish by replacing the sausage called for with fresh vegetables. It can be easily assembled the night before a busy day. Prepare a quick fruit salad while it's baking the next morning.
—Kate Hilts, Fairbanks, Alaska

1	loaf (1 pound) Italian bread, cut into 1/2-inch cubes
1	can (14-1/2 ounces) diced tomatoes, undrained
1	package (10 ounces) frozen chopped spinach, thawed and squeezed dry
1	cup chopped fresh mushrooms
1	cup (4 ounces) shredded part-skim mozzarella cheese
1/2	cup chopped green pepper
1/2	cup chopped zucchini
2	green onions, chopped
1	teaspoon dried basil
1/2	teaspoon dried oregano
1	cup fat-free milk
1	cup egg substitute
1	teaspoon salt-free seasoning blend
1/4	teaspoon pepper

In a large bowl, combine the first 10 ingredients. Transfer to a 13-in. x 9-in. baking dish coated with cooking spray.

In a small bowl, combine the milk, egg substitute, seasoning blend and pepper; pour over the vegetable mixture. Cover and refrigerate for 2 hours or overnight.

Remove from the refrigerator 30 minutes before baking. Cover and bake at 425° for 15 minutes. Uncover; bake 15 minutes longer or until a knife inserted near the center comes out clean. **YIELD: 16 SERVINGS.**

NUTRITION FACTS: 1 serving equals 128 calories, 3 g fat (0 saturated fat), 5 mg cholesterol, 292 mg sodium, 18 carbohydrate, 2 g fiber, 8 g protein. **DIABETIC EXCHANGES:** 1 starch, 1 vegetable, 1/2 meat.

homemade egg substitute (LC) (ML)

It's a cinch to whip up this easy egg substitute. Use this in place of whole eggs to cut out fat without losing any protein. It works great for omelets filled with veggies.
—Taste of Home Test Kitchen

2	large egg whites, lightly beaten
1	tablespoon nonfat dry milk powder
1	teaspoon canola oil
4	drops yellow food coloring, optional

In a small bowl, whisk the egg whites, milk powder and oil until well blended. Add food coloring if desired. **YIELD: 1/4 CUP EGG SUBSTITUTE EQUIVALENT TO 1 LARGE EGG, 1 SERVING.**

NUTRITION FACTS: 1/4 cup equals 100 calories, 5 g fat (0.55 g saturated fat), 1 mg cholesterol, 150 mg sodium, 5 g carbohydrate, 0 fiber, 10 g protein. **DIABETIC EXCHANGES:** 1 lean meat, 1 fat.

Editor's Note: The cholesterol in 1 large whole fresh egg is 213 mg.

low-cholesterol pancakes

low-cholesterol pancakes (LC) (ML)

When my husband and I developed high cholesterol, I found this wonderful way to convert our favorite pancake recipe. These pancakes are light, tender and slightly sweet.
—Dorothy Anne Adams, Valier, Montana

1	cup all-purpose flour
3	tablespoons sugar
1-1/2	teaspoons baking powder
1/2	teaspoon baking soda
1	cup buttermilk
1/4	cup canola oil
1	teaspoon vanilla extract
3	egg whites

In a small bowl, combine the first four ingredients. In another bowl, combine the buttermilk, oil and vanilla; add to dry ingredients. In a large bowl, beat egg whites until soft peaks form; fold into batter.

Pour batter by 1/4 cupfuls onto a hot griddle coated with cooking spray. Turn when bubbles form on top of pancakes. Cook until second side is lightly browned. **YIELD: 12 PANCAKES.**

NUTRITION FACTS: 1 pancake equals 104 calories, 5 g fat (0 saturated fat), 1 mg cholesterol, 149 mg sodium, 12 g carbohydrate, 0 fiber, 3 g protein. **DIABETIC EXCHANGES:** 1 starch, 1 fat.

berry blintzes

berry blintzes 🅜🅛

Biting into these delicately thin pancake packets sets off an explosion of flavors with every mouthful. The berries bring a burst of fruity sweetness to the creamy cheese filling. Blintzes make a luxurious breakfast or brunch.
—*Kristine Wright, St. Joseph, Michigan*

4	egg whites
1	cup fat-free milk
1/2	cup all-purpose flour
1	tablespoon sugar
1/8	teaspoon salt
1	cup part-skim ricotta cheese
4	ounces reduced-fat cream cheese
3/4	cup reduced-fat sour cream, *divided*
2	tablespoons sugar
1	tablespoon plus 2 teaspoons toasted wheat germ, *divided*
1	teaspoon vanilla extract
1	tablespoon butter, melted
1	cup unsweetened blueberries
1/2	cup unsweetened raspberries
1/2	cup unsweetened sliced strawberries

In a large bowl, combine the egg whites and milk. Combine the flour, sugar and salt; add to milk mixture and mix well. Cover and refrigerate for 1 hour.

Heat a lightly greased 8-in. nonstick skillet over medium heat; pour 1/4 cup batter into the center of skillet. Lift and tilt pan to coat bottom evenly. Cook until top appears dry; turn and cook 15-20 seconds longer. Remove to a wire rack. Repeat with remaining batter, greasing skillet as needed. When cool, stack crepes with waxed paper or paper towels in between.

For filling, in a small bowl, beat ricotta and cream until smooth. Beat in 1/2 cup sour cream, sugar, 1 tablespoon wheat germ and vanilla until blended. Spoon about 1/4 cup onto each blintze; fold ends and sides over filling.

Arrange blintzes folded side down in a 13-in. x 9-in. baking dish; brush with melted butter. Cover and bake at 350° for 10-15 minutes or until heated through. Top each blintze with berries and dollop of remaining sour cream. Sprinkle with remaining wheat germ. YIELD: 8 SERVINGS.

NUTRITION FACTS: 1 serving equals 210 calories, 9 g fat (6 g saturated fat), 30 mg cholesterol, 194 mg sodium, 22 g carbohydrate, 2 g fiber, 11 g protein. DIABETIC EXCHANGES: 1 lean meat, 1 fruit, 1/2 starch.

apple-cinnamon oatmeal mix 🅛🅕 🅜🅛

Oatmeal is a staple at our house. It's a warm, nutritious start to the day that keeps us going until lunch. We used to buy boxed oatmeal mixes, but we think our homemade version is better! Feel free to substitute raisins or other dried fruit for the apples.
—*Lynne Van Wagenen, Salt Lake City, Utah*

6	cups quick-cooking oats
1-1/3	cups nonfat dry milk powder
1	cup dried apples, diced
1/4	cup sugar
1/4	cup packed brown sugar
1	tablespoon ground cinnamon
1	teaspoon salt
1/4	teaspoon ground cloves

ADDITIONAL INGREDIENT (for each serving):

1/2	cup water

In a large bowl, combine the first eight ingredients. Store in an airtight container in a cool dry place for up to 6 months. YIELD: 8 CUPS TOTAL.

TO PREPARE OATMEAL: Shake mix well. In a small saucepan, bring water to a boil; slowly stir in 1/2 cup mix. Cook and stir over medium heat for 1 minute. Remove from the heat. Cover and let stand for 1 minute or until oatmeal reaches desired consistency. YIELD: 1 SERVING.

NUTRITION FACTS: 1 serving equals 176 calories, 2 g fat (trace saturated fat), 1 mg cholesterol, 185 mg sodium, 33 g carbohydrate, 4 g fiber, 7 g protein. DIABETIC EXCHANGE: 2 starch.

apple-cinnamon oatmeal mix

baked blueberry (ML) french toast

This entree makes a mouth-watering start to any morning. Since you can use fresh or frozen berries, it's great any time of year.

—*Suzanne Strocsher, Bothell, Washington*

24	slices day-old French bread (1/2 inch thick)
1	package (8 ounces) reduced-fat cream cheese, cubed
2/3	cup fat-free milk
1/2	cup reduced-fat sour cream
1/2	cup fat-free plain yogurt
1/3	cup maple syrup
1	teaspoon vanilla extract
1	teaspoon ground nutmeg
1/2	teaspoon ground cinnamon
2	cups egg substitute
2	cups fresh *or* frozen blueberries
2	tablespoons confectioners' sugar

Place 12 slices of bread in a 13-in. x 9-in. baking dish coated with cooking spray. In a blender or food processor, combine cream cheese, milk, sour cream, yogurt, syrup, vanilla, nutmeg and cinnamon. Add egg substitute; cover and process until smooth.

Pour half of the egg mixture over bread; sprinkle with blueberries. Top with the remaining bread and egg mixture. Cover and refrigerate for 8 hours or overnight.

Remove from the refrigerator 30 minutes before baking. Cover and bake at 350° for 30 minutes. Uncover; bake 20-30 minutes longer or until a knife inserted near the center comes out clean. Let stand for 10 minutes before serving. Dust with confectioners' sugar. **YIELD: 12 SERVINGS.**

NUTRITION FACTS: 2 slices equals 228 calories, 5 g fat (3 g saturated fat), 14 mg cholesterol, 391 mg sodium, 33 g carbohydrate, 2 g fiber, 11 g protein. **DIABETIC EXCHANGES:** 1 starch, 1 fat-free milk, 1/2 fruit.

Editor's Note: *If using frozen blueberries, do not thaw before adding to batter.*

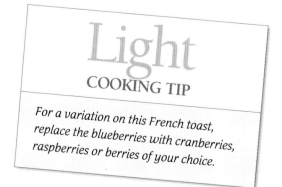

Light COOKING TIP

For a variation on this French toast, replace the blueberries with cranberries, raspberries or berries of your choice.

green 'n' gold (LC) (ML) egg bake

You need only five ingredients to assemble this tasty casserole. The delicious spinach flavor is welcome at breakfast or dinner.

—*Muriel Paceleo, Montgomery, New York*

1	cup seasoned bread crumbs, *divided*
2	packages (10 ounces *each*) frozen chopped spinach, thawed and squeezed dry
3	cups (24 ounces) 4% cottage cheese
1/2	cup grated Romano *or* Parmesan cheese
5	eggs

Sprinkle 1/4 cup seasoned bread crumbs into a greased 8-in. square baking dish. Bake at 350° for 3-5 minutes or until golden brown.

Meanwhile, in a large bowl, combine the spinach, cottage cheese, Romano cheese, three eggs and remaining crumbs. Spread over the baked crumbs. Beat remaining eggs; pour over spinach mixture.

Bake, uncovered, at 350° for 45 minutes or until a knife inserted near the center comes out clean. Let stand for 5-10 minutes before serving. **YIELD: 9 SERVINGS.**

NUTRITION FACTS: 1/2-cup serving (prepared with fat-free cottage cheese and egg substitute) equals 181 calories, 6 g fat (2 g saturated fat), 127 mg cholesterol, 808 mg sodium, 15 g carbohydrate, 2 g fiber, 18 g protein. **DIABETIC EXCHANGES:** 2 lean meat, 1 starch.

green 'n' gold egg bake

crustless spinach quiche (LC) (ML)

My daughter is a vegetarian, so I eliminated the ham called for in the original recipe. Wedges of this healthful quiche make a fast and delicious brunch, lunch or supper.

—Vicki Schrupp, St. Cloud, Minnesota

- 3 ounces reduced-fat cream cheese, softened
- 1 cup fat-free milk
- 1 cup egg substitute
- 1/4 teaspoon pepper
- 3 cups (12 ounces) shredded reduced-fat cheddar cheese
- 3 cups frozen chopped spinach, thawed and squeezed dry
- 1 cup frozen chopped broccoli, thawed and well drained
- 1 small onion, finely chopped
- 5 fresh mushrooms, sliced

In a small bowl, beat the cream cheese. Add the milk, egg substitute and pepper; beat until smooth. Stir in the remaining ingredients.

Transfer to a 10-in. quiche pan coated with cooking spray. Bake at 350° for 45-50 minutes or until a knife inserted near the center comes out clean. YIELD: 8 SERVINGS.

NUTRITION FACTS: 1 piece equals 151 calories, 5 g fat (0 saturated fat), 14 mg cholesterol, 404 mg sodium, 8 g carbohydrate, 2 g fiber, 18 g protein. **DIABETIC EXCHANGES:** 1 starch, 1 meat.

sausage egg puff

I stir up this full-flavored brunch dish at night so it's ready to bake up light and fluffy the next morning when time is tight. Turkey sausage links and egg substitute give this dish a high protein score.

—Tammy Lamb, Campbellsville, Kentucky

- 1 package (12 ounces) breakfast turkey sausage links, casings removed
- 1 cup reduced-fat biscuit/baking mix
- 1 cup (4 ounces) shredded reduced-fat cheddar cheese
- 1 teaspoon ground mustard
- 1 teaspoon Italian seasoning
- 1 cup egg substitute
- 2 eggs
- 2 cups fat-free milk

In a large skillet, crumble turkey sausage and cook until no longer pink; drain. In a large bowl, combine the biscuit mix, cheese, mustard and Italian seasoning; add sausage.

In another bowl, whisk the egg substitute, eggs and milk; stir into the sausage mixture. Transfer to a shallow 2-qt. baking dish coated with cooking spray. Cover and refrigerate overnight.

Remove from the refrigerator 30 minutes before baking. Bake, uncovered, at 350° for 50-55 minutes or until a knife inserted near the center comes out clean. YIELD: 6 SERVINGS.

NUTRITION FACTS: 1 serving equals 324 calories, 14 g fat (4 g saturated fat), 134 mg cholesterol, 1,111 mg sodium, 19 g carbohydrate, trace fiber, 30 g protein. **DIABETIC EXCHANGES:** 4 lean meat, 1 starch, 1/2 fat.

crustless spinach quiche

Light
COOKING TIP

Are you a vegetarian? If you consume eggs but not meat, then try substituting soy crumbles for the turkey sausage called for in the recipe above.

apple pancakes  (LF) (ML)

My husband is a hearty eater with a penchant for pancakes. We are both diabetic, so I revised my recipe to fit our dietary needs.
—*Fern Motzinger, Omaha, Nebraska*

  2 cups reduced-fat biscuit/baking mix
Sugar substitute equivalent to 2 teaspoons sugar
  1 teaspoon baking powder
  1 teaspoon ground cinnamon
1/4 teaspoon salt
1/4 cup egg substitute
  1 cup fat-free milk
  2 teaspoons vanilla extract
  1 tart apple, peeled and grated

In a large bowl, combine the biscuit mix, sweetener, baking powder, cinnamon and salt. In a small bowl, combine the egg substitute, milk and vanilla; stir into dry ingredients. Fold in apple.

Pour batter by 1/4 cupfuls onto a hot skillet coated with cooking spray; turn when bubbles form on top. Cook until second side is golden brown. **YIELD: 10 SERVINGS.**

NUTRITION FACTS: 1 pancake equals 117 calories, 2 g fat (0 saturated fat), 1 mg cholesterol, 420 mg sodium, 21 g carbohydrate, 0 fiber, 3 g protein. **DIABETIC EXCHANGES:** 1-1/2 starch, 1/2 fat.

french toast fingers (ML)

Kids love French toast sticks, but restaurant versions are often deep fried. Save yourself the guilt—and a little money, too—by preparing this healthful alternative at home.
—*Mavis Diment, Marcus, Iowa*

  2 eggs
1/4 cup milk
1/4 teaspoon salt
1/2 cup strawberry preserves
  8 slices day-old white bread
Confectioners' sugar, optional

In a small bowl, whisk eggs, milk and salt; set aside. Spread preserves on four slices of bread; top with the remaining bread. Trim crusts; cut each sandwich into three strips.

Dip both sides in egg mixture. Cook on a lightly greased hot griddle for 2 minutes on each side or until golden brown. Dust with confectioners' sugar if desired. **YIELD: 4 SERVINGS.**

NUTRITION FACTS: Three French toast fingers (prepared with egg substitute, fat-free milk and sugar-free preserves and without confectioners' sugar) equals 235 calories, 4 g fat (0 saturated fat), 2 mg cholesterol, 500 mg sodium, 42 g carbohydrate, 0 fiber, 10 g protein. **DIABETIC EXCHANGES:** 2 starch, 1 meat, 1/2 fruit.

french toast fingers

vegetarian burritos (LF) (ML)

Our daughter loves to help out in the kitchen, so I try to choose dishes that are easy to follow. Just six ingredients, including convenient salsa, create the zippy filling in these speedy burritos.
—*Ruth Behm, Defiance, Ohio*

 10 eggs
1/2 teaspoon salt, optional
1/8 teaspoon pepper
  1 cup salsa
1/4 cup chopped onion
  1 cup (4 ounces) shredded cheddar cheese
  8 flour tortillas (6 to 7 inches), warmed

In a large bowl, beat the eggs, salt if desired and pepper. Pour into a skillet that has been coated with cooking spray.

Cook and stir over medium heat until eggs are partially set. Add salsa and onion; cook and stir until eggs are completely set. Sprinkle with cheese. Spoon about 1/2 cup down the center of each tortilla; fold ends and sides over filling. Serve immediately. **YIELD: 8 SERVINGS.**

NUTRITION FACTS: 1 burrito (prepared with egg substitute, reduced-fat cheese and fat-free tortillas and without salt) equals 154 calories, 3 g fat (2 g saturated fat), 10 mg cholesterol, 744 mg sodium, 17 g carbohydrate, 2 g fiber, 13 g protein. **DIABETIC EXCHANGES:** 1-1/2 starch, 1 meat, 1 vegetable, 1/2 fat.

appetizers, snacks & breads

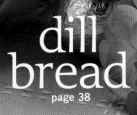

dill bread

page 38

seafood nachos

seafood nachos

I love seafood and sometimes order the seafood nacho appetizer at our local Mexican restaurant as my entree. I've tried many times to duplicate those tasty morsels at home—this recipe comes close.

—Linda McKee, Big Prairie, Ohio

30	tortilla chips	2	tablespoons finely chopped onion
1	package (8 ounces) imitation crabmeat, chopped	1/4	teaspoon dill weed
1/4	cup reduced-fat sour cream	1	cup (4 ounces) shredded reduced-fat cheddar cheese
1/4	cup reduced-fat mayonnaise	1/4	cup sliced ripe olives
		1/4	teaspoon paprika

Arrange tortilla chips in a single layer on an ungreased baking sheet. In a bowl, combine the crab, sour cream, mayonnaise, onion and dill; spoon about 1 tablespoon onto each chip. Sprinkle with cheese, olives and paprika. Bake at 350° for 6-8 minutes or until cheese is melted. **YIELD: 6 SERVINGS.**

NUTRITION FACTS: 5 nachos equals 190 calories, 9 g fat (3 g saturated fat), 25 mg cholesterol, 531 mg sodium, 16 g carbohydrate, 1 g fiber, 13 g protein. **DIABETIC EXCHANGES:** 1 starch, 1 lean meat, 1 fat.

Light COOKING TIP

Imitation crabmeat, also called surimi, is fish that is shaped, flavored and colored to resemble crab. It is typically made from Alaskan pollock, a lean, firm fish with a delicate flavor. Both natural and artificial flavors are used as well as artificial coloring.

rustic round herb bread

rustic round herb bread ML

I've had this bread recipe for years. It takes only a few minutes to stir together. Wedges are marvelous served warm and are great with hearty vegetable soup.
— *Patricia Vatta, Norwood, Ontario*

- 2 cups all-purpose flour
- 1 cup (4 ounces) shredded reduced-fat cheddar cheese
- 1 tablespoon sugar
- 2 teaspoons baking powder
- 1/2 teaspoon baking soda
- 1/2 teaspoon salt
- 1/2 teaspoon rubbed sage
- 1/2 teaspoon dried thyme
- 1/2 teaspoon dill weed
- 3 tablespoons cold butter
- 1 egg
- 1/2 cup fat-free plain yogurt
- 1/2 cup fat-free milk
- 1/2 teaspoon poppy seeds

In a large bowl, combine the first nine ingredients. Cut in butter until mixture resembles fine crumbs. In another bowl, whisk the egg, yogurt and milk. Stir into dry ingredients until just moistened.

Spoon into a 9-in. round baking pan coated with cooking spray. Sprinkle with poppy seeds.

Bake at 400° for 20-25 minutes or until golden brown. Cool in pan on a wire rack. Cut into wedges. **YIELD: 10 SERVINGS.**

NUTRITION FACTS: 1 wedge equals 185 calories, 7 g fat (4 g saturated fat), 39 mg cholesterol, 379 mg sodium, 23 g carbohydrate, 1 g fiber, 7 g protein. **DIABETIC EXCHANGES:** 1-1/2 starch, 1 fat.

spinach artichoke spread LF LC LS ML

This tempting baked spinach and artichoke spread makes a great appetizer for any occasion. Serve it warm from the oven with reduced-fat crackers.
— *Nancy Farmer, Jordan, Arkansas*

- 1 package (8 ounces) reduced-fat cream cheese, softened
- 1 cup (8 ounces) reduced-fat sour cream
- 1 package (10 ounces) frozen chopped spinach, thawed and squeezed dry
- 1 package (9 ounces) frozen artichoke hearts, thawed, drained and chopped
- 2 teaspoons lemon juice
- 1/2 teaspoon salt-free seasoning blend
- 1/2 teaspoon pepper
- Reduced-fat crackers

In a large bowl, beat cream cheese and sour cream until smooth. Stir in spinach and artichokes. Add the lemon juice, seasoning blend and pepper.

Transfer to a 9-in. pie plate coated with cooking spray. Bake at 350° for 20-30 minutes or until mixture bubbles around the edges. Serve warm with crackers. **YIELD: 4 CUPS.**

NUTRITION FACTS: 1/4 cup (calculated without crackers) equals 49 calories, 3 g fat (0 saturated fat), 10 mg cholesterol, 82 mg sodium, 3 g carbohydrate, 2 g fiber, 3 g protein. **DIABETIC EXCHANGES:** 1 vegetable, 1/2 fat.

chili popcorn ML

I came up with this fun, deliciously different seasoned popcorn to provide a snack for my extended family of high school actors when I was teaching drama. It's inexpensive and easy—a great way to take the edge off feisty appetites. This is an irresistible pop-in-your-mouth treat.
— *Patsie Ronk, Galveston, Indiana*

- 3 quarts popped popcorn
- 2 tablespoons butter, melted
- 1 tablespoon Dijon mustard
- 2 teaspoons chili powder
- 1/4 teaspoon *each* salt and ground cumin

Place the popcorn in a large bowl. Combine the remaining ingredients. Drizzle over popcorn; toss until well coated. **YIELD: 3 QUARTS.**

NUTRITION FACTS: 1 cup equals 68 calories, 4 g fat (0 saturated fat), 0 cholesterol, 204 mg sodium, 7 g carbohydrate, 0 fiber, 1 g protein. **DIABETIC EXCHANGES:** 1/2 starch, 1/2 fat.

apple salsa with cinnamon chips (LF) (LS) (ML)

For a sweet delight that's sure to be requested at all your parties, try this appetizer. The salsa offers good-for-you fruits, and the crunchy home-baked chips are a healthful alternative to store-bought brands.

—Courtney Fons, Brighton, Michigan

6	flour tortillas (8 inches)
3	tablespoons sugar
1-1/2	teaspoons ground cinnamon
4	cups finely chopped tart apples (about 2 medium)
1	cup finely chopped ripe pear
1/2	cup quartered seedless red grapes
1/2	cup chopped celery
1/4	cup chopped walnuts
3	tablespoons orange juice
1	tablespoon brown sugar
2	teaspoons grated orange peel

Coat both sides of each tortilla with cooking spray. Combine the sugar and cinnamon; sprinkle over both sides of tortillas.

Cut each into eight wedges. Place on baking sheets. Bake at 400° for 4-5 minutes or until crisp.

Meanwhile, for the salsa, in a small bowl, combine the remaining ingredients. Serve with the cinnamon chips. YIELD: 12 SERVINGS.

NUTRITION FACTS: 1/2 cup salsa with 4 chips equals 141 calories, 3 g fat (trace saturated fat), 0 cholesterol, 129 mg sodium, 26 g carbohydrate, 1 g fiber, 3 g protein. DIABETIC EXCHANGES: 1 starch, 1 fruit, 1/2 fat.

apple salsa with cinnamon chips

strawberry dip (LC) (LS) (ML)

After a card game one evening, our hostess served graham crackers spread with prepared strawberry cream cheese. The flavor combination was scrumptious. So I decided to make a similar blend using fresh berries. Guests appreciate this simple treat.

—Carol Gaus, Itasca, Illinois

1	package (8 ounces) cream cheese, softened
2	tablespoons honey
1	teaspoon vanilla extract
1	pint fresh strawberries, sliced

Graham crackers

In a large bowl, beat the cream cheese, honey and vanilla until smooth. Add strawberries; beat for 1 minute. Serve with graham crackers. YIELD: 2 CUPS.

NUTRITION FACTS: 2 tablespoons dip (prepared with reduced-fat cream cheese) equals 82 calories, 5 g fat (3 g saturated fat), 16 mg cholesterol, 84 mg sodium, 6 g carbohydrate, trace fiber, 3 g protein. DIABETIC EXCHANGES: 1 fat, 1/2 fruit.

stuffed mushrooms (LF) (LC) (ML)

I first tasted these fun mushroom bites at a support group meeting for diabetics. I couldn't believe how yummy they were. Since then, I've shared the recipe with friends and co-workers.

—Beth Ann Howard, Verona, Pennsylvania

1	pound large fresh mushrooms
3	tablespoons seasoned bread crumbs
3	tablespoons fat-free sour cream
2	tablespoons grated Parmesan cheese
2	tablespoons minced chives
2	tablespoons reduced-fat mayonnaise
2	teaspoons balsamic vinegar
2	to 3 drops hot pepper sauce, optional

Remove stems from mushrooms; set caps aside. Chop stems, reserving 1/3 cup (discard remaining stems or save for another use). In a bowl, combine the bread crumbs, sour cream, Parmesan cheese, chives, mayonnaise, vinegar, hot pepper sauce if desired and reserved mushroom stems; mix well.

Place the mushroom caps on a baking sheet coated with cooking spray; stuff with the crumb mixture. Boil 4-6 in. from the heat for 5-7 minutes or until lightly browned. YIELD: 6 SERVINGS.

NUTRITION FACTS: 3 stuffed mushrooms equals 66 calories, 3 g fat (1 g saturated fat), 4 mg cholesterol, 173 mg sodium, 8 g carbohydrate, 1 g fiber, 4 g protein. DIABETIC EXCHANGES: 1/2 starch, 1/2 fat.

warm fruit medley ⓛⒻ ⓛⓈ ⓂⓁ

The gently spiced snack our home economists created is comfort food at its healthiest. Spotlighting wonderful fruit like pears, cherries, apricots, pineapple and cranberries, it makes a beautiful compote that's perfect for a brunch or buffet.

—Taste of Home Test Kitchen

2	tablespoons sugar
2	tablespoons cornstarch
1/2	teaspoon ground ginger
1/4	teaspoon ground allspice
1	cup apricot nectar
2	tablespoons butter, melted
6	cups sliced peeled fresh pears
1	can (15 ounces) reduced-sugar apricot halves, drained and halved
1	can (15 ounces) pitted dark sweet cherries, drained
1	can (8 ounces) unsweetened pineapple chunks, drained
3/4	cup dried cranberries

In a large bowl, combine the sugar, cornstarch, ginger and allspice. Stir in nectar and butter until smooth. Add fruit; stir to coat.

Pour into a 3-qt. baking dish coated with cooking spray. Cover and bake at 350° for 30 minutes. Uncover; bake 10 minutes longer or until hot and bubbly. Serve warm. **YIELD: 12 SERVINGS.**

NUTRITION FACTS: 3/4 cup equals 150 calories, trace fat (trace saturated fat), 0 cholesterol, 4 mg sodium, 39 g carbohydrate, 4 g fiber, 1 g protein. **DIABETIC EXCHANGES:** 2 fruit, 1/2 fat.

warm fruit medley

baked spinach dip loaf

baked spinach dip loaf ⓛⒸ

A crusty, round sourdough loaf provides not only dippers but also the serving bowl for this popular treat.

—Frieda Meding, Trochu, Alberta

2	packages (8 ounces *each*) cream cheese, softened
1	cup mayonnaise
1	package (10 ounces) frozen chopped spinach, thawed and squeezed dry
1	cup (4 ounces) shredded cheddar cheese
1	can (8 ounces) water chestnuts, drained and chopped
5	bacon strips, cooked and crumbled
1	green onion, chopped
2	teaspoons dill weed
1	garlic clove, minced
1/2	teaspoon seasoned salt
1/8	teaspoon pepper
1	unsliced round loaf (1 pound) sourdough bread

Raw vegetables

In a large bowl, beat cream cheese and mayonnaise. Stir in the spinach, cheese, water chestnuts, bacon, onion and seasonings.

Cut a 1-1/2-in. slice off top of the bread; set aside. Carefully hollow out bottom, leaving a 1/2-in. shell. Cube removed bread and set aside. Fill the shell with spinach dip; replace top. Wrap in heavy-duty foil; place on a baking sheet.

Bake at 375° for 1-1/4 to 1-1/2 hours or until dip is heated through. Open foil carefully. Serve warm with bread cubes and vegetables. **YIELD: 4-1/2 CUPS.**

NUTRITION FACTS: 1/4 cup dip (calculated without bread cubes or vegetables) equals 105 calories, 7 g fat (4 g saturated fat), 20 mg cholesterol, 303 mg sodium, 6 g carbohydrate, 1 g fiber, 6 g protein. **DIABETIC EXCHANGES:** 2 vegetable, 1 fat.

Editor's Note: *Reduced-fat or fat-free mayonnaise is not recommended for this recipe.*

bright blueberry muffins (ML)

Dried cranberries are a nice alternative to the blueberries in these tasty muffins. My diabetic friends think these are great.
—Pat Byble, Springhill, West Virginia

1/2	cup reduced-fat margarine
Sugar substitute equivalent to 1 cup sugar	
2	eggs
1/4	cup honey
1	teaspoon vanilla extract
2	cups all-purpose flour
2	teaspoons baking powder
1/4	teaspoon salt
1/2	cup 2% milk
1	cup fresh *or* frozen blueberries

In a large bowl, beat margarine and sugar substitute until light and fluffy. Add eggs, one at a time, beating well after each addition. Beat in honey and vanilla. Combine the flour, baking powder and salt; add to egg mixture alternately with milk, beating just until combined. Gently fold in blueberries.

Coat the muffin cups with the cooking spray or line with paper liners; fill three-fourths full with batter. Bake at 350° for 20-25 minutes or until a toothpick inserted near the center comes out clean. Cool for 5 minutes before removing from pan to a wire rack. Serve warm. YIELD: 1 DOZEN.

NUTRITION FACTS: 1 muffin equals 171 calories, 6 g fat (1 g saturated fat), 36 mg cholesterol, 192 mg sodium, 26 g carbohydrate, 1 g fiber, 4 g protein. DIABETIC EXCHANGES: 1 starch, 1 fat, 1/2 fruit.

Editor's Note: If using frozen blueberries, do not thaw before adding to batter.

cheesy bagel bites (LF) (ML)

Here's a simple recipe that adds zippy flavor to everyday bagels. I recommend this speedy method for filling up a snack tray in a nutritious way...and emptying it even quicker!
—Becky Ruff, McGregor, Iowa

1/3	cup reduced-fat mayonnaise
1/4	cup grated Parmesan cheese
1	tablespoon prepared mustard
2	green onions, finely chopped
1/4	teaspoon garlic powder
3	whole wheat bagels, split and toasted

In a small bowl, combine the mayonnaise, Parmesan cheese, mustard, onions and garlic powder. Spread over bagels.

Place on a the baking sheet. Broil 4-6 in. from the heat for 1-2 minutes or until golden brown and bubbly. Cut each bagel half into six pieces. YIELD: 12 SERVINGS.

NUTRITION FACTS: 3 pieces equals 105 calories, 3 g fat (1 g saturated fat), 4 mg cholesterol, 248 mg sodium, 16 g carbohydrate, 3 g fiber, 4 g protein. DIABETIC EXCHANGES: 1 starch, 1/2 fat.

flavorful herb bread

flavorful herb bread (LF) (LS) (ML)

This lovely low-sodium loaf gets its delicious flavor from a handful of fragrant herbs.
—Nancy Zimmerman, Cape May Court House, New Jersey

1	package (1/4 ounce) active dry yeast
1	cup warm water (110° to 115°)
3	tablespoons sugar
2	tablespoons butter, melted
1	tablespoon dried parsley flakes
1-1/2	teaspoons dried basil
1/2	teaspoon dried oregano
1/2	teaspoon dried thyme
1/4	teaspoon garlic powder
2-1/2	to 3 cups all-purpose flour

In a large bowl, dissolve yeast in water. Stir in the sugar, butter, parsley, basil, oregano, thyme, garlic powder and 1 cup flour. Beat until smooth. Stir in enough remaining flour to form a soft dough. Turn onto a lightly floured surface; knead until smooth and elastic, about 5-6 minutes. Place in a large bowl coated with cooking spray, turning once to coat top. Cover and let rise in a warm place until doubled, about 1 hour.

Punch dough down; turn onto a lightly floured surface. Shape into loaf. Place in a 9-in. x 5-in. loaf pan coated with cooking spray. Cover and let rise in a warm place until doubled, about 30 minutes. Bake at 375° for 30-35 minutes or until golden brown. Remove from pan to a wire rack to cool. YIELD: 1 LOAF (16 SLICES).

NUTRITION FACTS: 1 slice equals 103 calories, 2 g fat (1 g saturated fat), 4 mg cholesterol, 16 mg sodium, 19 g carbohydrate, 1 g fiber, 2 g protein. DIABETIC EXCHANGES: 1 starch, 1/2 fat.

potato rolls

grilled seasoned shrimp

A marinade using balsamic vinegar, lemon juice and Italian dressing boosts the flavor of these tender shrimp. I serve these delightful snacks chilled.
> —Diane Harrison, Mechanicsburg, Pennsylvania

1-1/2	pounds uncooked large shrimp
1	small red onion, sliced and separated into rings
1/4	cup prepared Italian salad dressing
2	green onions, chopped
2	tablespoons lemon juice
2	tablespoons balsamic vinegar
2	tablespoons olive oil
3	garlic cloves, minced

Salt and coarsely ground pepper to taste, optional

Peel and devein shrimp, leaving tails intact if desired. Coat a grill rack with cooking spray before starting the grill.

Grill the shrimp, covered, over indirect medium heat for 2-3 minutes on each side or until shrimp turn pink. Cool; cover and refrigerate until chilled.

In a large resealable plastic bag, combine the remaining ingredients; add shrimp. Seal bag and turn to coat; refrigerate for at least 2 hours. Serve with a slotted spoon. **YIELD: 4 SERVINGS.**

NUTRITION FACTS: 3 large shrimp (prepared with fat-free salad dressing and without salt) equals 267 calories, 10 g fat (2 g saturated fat), 259 mg cholesterol, 470 mg sodium, 7 g carbohydrate, 1 g fiber, 35 g protein. **DIABETIC EXCHANGES:** 4 very lean meat, 2 fat, 1/2 fruit.

potato rolls (LF) (ML)

What better time to shape rolls into cloverleafs than for the celebration of St. Patrick's Day? I found this recipe in a magazine several years ago. These rolls are well received at fellowship dinners and are also popular at home. They are the lightest and tastiest rolls I make.
> —Beatrice McGrath, Norridgewock, Maine

1	package (1/4 ounce) active dry yeast
1/4	cup warm water (110° to 115°)
1	cup warm milk (110° to 115°)
1/4	cup shortening
1/2	cup warm mashed potatoes
1	egg
1/4	cup sugar
1-1/4	teaspoons salt
4	cups all-purpose flour

In a large bowl, dissolve yeast in water. Add the milk, shortening, potatoes, egg, sugar, salt and 2 cups flour. Beat until smooth. Add enough remaining flour to form a soft dough.

Turn onto a floured surface; knead until smooth and elastic, about 6-8 minutes. Place in a greased bowl, turning once to grease top. Cover and let rise in a warm place until doubled, about 1 hour.

Punch dough down and divide in half. Divide each half into 36 pieces; shape into balls. Place three balls each into greased muffin cups. Cover and let rise in a warm place until doubled, about 30 minutes.

Bake at 400° for 12-15 minutes or until golden. Remove to wire racks. Serve warm. **YIELD: 2 DOZEN.**

NUTRITION FACTS: 1 roll (prepared with fat-free milk) equals 115 calories, 3 g fat (0 saturated fat), 9 mg cholesterol, 142 mg sodium, 19 g carbohydrate, 0 fiber, 3 g protein. **DIABETIC EXCHANGES:** 1 starch, 1 fat.

grilled seasoned shrimp

creamy herb appetizer pockets

Place 1 rounded tablespoon of filling in the center of each square. Fold in half, forming triangles. Crimp edges to seal; trim if necessary. Place on ungreased baking sheets. Bake at 375° for 10-15 minutes or until golden brown. Serve warm. **YIELD: 2 DOZEN.**

NUTRITION FACTS: 2 pockets equals 96 calories, 5 g fat (2 g saturated fat), 7 mg cholesterol, 302 mg sodium, 10 g carbohydrate, trace fiber, 3 g protein. **DIABETIC EXCHANGES:** 1 starch, 1 fat.

Editor's Note: This recipe was tested with Boursin Light Cheese Spread with garlic and fine herbs. One carton contains about 7 tablespoons of cheese spread.

creamy herb appetizer pockets LC ML

I combined a creamy cheese sauce and an artichoke dip to come up with these bite-size morsels. The filling is tucked into triangles made from refrigerated crescent roll dough—it's the perfect no-mess appetizer!
—Tina Scarpaci, Chandler, Arizona

1	carton (4.4 ounces) reduced-fat garlic-herb cheese spread
4	ounces reduced-fat cream cheese
2	tablespoons half-and-half cream
1	garlic clove, minced
1	tablespoon dried basil
1	teaspoon dried thyme
1/2	teaspoon celery salt
1/4	teaspoon dill weed
1/4	teaspoon salt
1/4	teaspoon pepper
3	to 4 drops hot pepper sauce
1/2	cup chopped canned water-packed artichoke hearts, rinsed and drained
1/4	cup chopped roasted red peppers
2	tubes (8 ounces *each*) refrigerated reduced-fat crescent rolls

In a small bowl, beat the cheese spread, cream cheese, cream and garlic until blended. Beat in the herbs, salt, pepper and hot pepper sauce. Fold in artichokes and red peppers. Cover and refrigerate for at least 1 hour.

Unroll both tubes of crescent roll dough. On a lightly floured surface, form each tube of dough into a long rectangle; seal seams and perforations. Roll each into a 16-in. x 12-in. rectangle. Cut lengthwise into four strips and width-wise into three strips; separate squares.

cauliflower hors d'oeuvres LF LC ML

These crispy baked tidbits are an appealing alternative to deep-fried fare. A coating of Parmesan cheese, Worcestershire sauce, basil and ground mustard infuses a burst of flavor into each bite. I make these nibblers for parties, and it's always the first plate to be emptied.
—Dorothy MacNeill, St. Petersburg, Florida

8	cups fresh cauliflowerets (3 pounds *each*)
1/2	cup egg substitute
2	tablespoons butter, melted
2	teaspoons Worcestershire sauce
1	teaspoon ground mustard
1	cup seasoned bread crumbs
1/3	cup grated Parmesan cheese
1/4	teaspoon dried basil
1/8	teaspoon salt
1/8	teaspoon pepper
1/8	teaspoon paprika

Meatless spaghetti sauce, warmed, optional

Place 1 in. of water and cauliflower in a saucepan; bring to a boil. Reduce heat; cover and simmer for 5 minutes. Drain and immediately place cauliflower in ice water. Drain and pat dry.

In a shallow bowl, combine the egg substitute, butter, Worcestershire sauce and mustard. In another bowl, combine bread crumbs, Parmesan cheese, basil, salt, pepper and paprika. Dip cauliflower into the egg mixture, then coat with crumb mixture.

Place in two ungreased 15-in. x 10-in. x 1-in. baking pans. Bake at 350° for 30-35 minutes or until golden. Serve with spaghetti sauce for dipping if desired. **YIELD: 14 SERVINGS.**

NUTRITION FACTS: 1/2 cup cauliflower equals 76 calories, 3 g fat (2 g saturated fat), 6 mg cholesterol, 319 mg sodium, 8 g carbohydrate, 2 g fiber, 4 g protein. **DIABETIC EXCHANGES:** 1 vegetable, 1/2 starch, 1/2 fat.

cheddar batter bread (LS) (ML)

I love batter breads because I can offer my family delicious homemade bread without the hassle of kneading and shaping the dough. This loaf is terrific with chili.

—Deb Keslar, Utica, Nebraska

2	cups all-purpose flour
2	tablespoons sugar
1	package (1/4 ounce) active dry yeast
1/4	teaspoon onion powder
1/4	teaspoon salt
1/4	teaspoon pepper
1	cup milk
2	tablespoons butter, softened
1	egg
1/2	cup cornmeal
3/4	cup shredded cheddar cheese

Additional cornmeal

In a large bowl, combine 1-1/2 cups flour, sugar, yeast, onion powder, salt and pepper. In a small saucepan, heat milk and butter to 120°-130°. Add to dry ingredients; beat until moistened. Add egg; beat on low speed for 30 seconds. Beat on high for 3 minutes. Stir in cornmeal and remaining flour. Stir in cheese (batter will be thick). Do not knead. Cover and let rise in a warm place until doubled, about 20 minutes.

Stir dough down. Grease an 8-in. x 4-in. loaf pan and sprinkle with additional cornmeal. Spoon batter into prepared

cheddar batter bread

spiced hot fruit

pan. Cover and let rise in a warm place until doubled, about 30 minutes.

Bake at 350° for 35-40 minutes or until golden brown. Cool for 10 minutes before removing from pan to a wire rack. Store in the refrigerator. YIELD: 1 LOAF (16 SLICES).

NUTRITION FACTS: 1 slice equals 125 calories, 4 g fat (2 g saturated fat), 24 mg cholesterol, 90 mg sodium, 18 g carbohydrate, 1 g fiber, 4 g protein. DIABETIC EXCHANGES: 1 starch, 1 fat.

spiced hot fruit (LF) (LS) (ML)

This recipe takes advantage of convenient canned fruit. Assembled in a flash, this crowd-pleasing compote is sparked with cinnamon and ginger.

—Irene Howard, Shenandoah, Iowa

2	cans (one 20 ounces, one 8 ounces) pineapple chunks
2	cans (15-1/4 ounces *each*) apricots, drained and quartered
1	can (29 ounces) sliced peaches, drained
1	can (29 ounces) pear halves, drained and quartered
3/4	cup packed brown sugar
1/4	cup butter, cubed
2	cinnamon sticks (3 inches)
1/2	teaspoon ground ginger

Drain pineapple, reserving juice. In an ungreased shallow 3-1/2-qt. baking dish, combine the pineapple, apricots, peaches and pears; set aside. In a saucepan, combine brown sugar, butter, cinnamon, ginger and reserved pineapple juice; bring to a boil. Reduce heat; simmer for 5 minutes. Discard cinnamon sticks. Pour over fruit.

Bake, uncovered, at 350° for 30 minutes or until heated through. Serve warm. YIELD: 10 CUPS.

NUTRITION FACTS: 1/3 cup equals 165 calories, 3 g fat (trace saturated fat), 0 cholesterol, 35 mg sodium, 37 g carbohydrate, 2 g fiber, 1 g protein. DIABETIC EXCHANGES: 2 fruit, 1/2 fat.

turkey quesadillas

Loaded with garden-fresh vegetables, this Mexican specialty is sure to be popular with the whole family. Plus, it's a snap to make on a busy weeknight.

—Wendy Greinke, Round Rock, Texas

1	pound lean ground turkey
1	cup chopped red onion
1	to 2 garlic cloves, minced
2	cups julienned zucchini
1	cup salsa
1	cup frozen corn
1	cup julienned sweet red pepper
1	can (4 ounces) chopped green chilies
2	tablespoons minced fresh cilantro
1/2	teaspoon dried oregano
1/2	teaspoon ground cumin
1/4	teaspoon salt
1/8	teaspoon cayenne pepper
8	flour tortillas (8 inches)
2	cups (8 ounces) shredded reduced-fat Mexican cheese blend

In a large nonstick skillet, cook the turkey, onion and the garlic over medium heat until meat is no longer pink; drain. Add zucchini, salsa, corn, red pepper and chilies. Reduce heat; cover and simmer until the vegetables are tender. Stir in seasonings.

For each quesadilla, place one tortilla in an ungreased nonstick skillet. Sprinkle with 1/4 cup cheese. Top with 1/2 cup filling, then sprinkle with another 1/4 cup cheese.

turkey quesadillas

raspberry lemon loaf

Cover with another tortilla. Cook over medium heat, carefully turning once, until lightly browned on both sides and the cheese begins to melt. Cut into eight wedges. YIELD: 4 QUESADILLAS (8 WEDGES EACH).

NUTRITION FACTS: 4 wedges equals 349 calories, 13 g fat (5 g saturated fat), 55 mg cholesterol, 771 mg sodium, 37 g carbohydrate, 3 g fiber, 24 g protein. **DIABETIC EXCHANGES:** 2 starch, 2 lean meat, 1-1/2 fat.

raspberry lemon loaf (ML)

This easy-to-prepare quick bread is flavored with tangy lemon peel and fresh raspberries. The loaf is refreshing as a snack, at breakfast...or any time of day.

—Carol Dodds, Aurora, Ontario

1-3/4	cups all-purpose flour
1/2	cup sugar
1	teaspoon baking powder
1/2	teaspoon baking soda
1/2	teaspoon salt
1	egg
2	egg whites
1	cup reduced-fat lemon yogurt
1/4	cup canola oil
2	teaspoons grated lemon peel
1	cup fresh raspberries

In a large bowl, combine the dry ingredients. In another bowl, whisk together the egg, egg whites, yogurt, oil and lemon peel. Add to the dry ingredients just until moistened. Fold in the raspberries.

Transfer to an 8-in. x 4-in. loaf pan coated with cooking spray. Bake at 350° for 60-65 minutes or until a toothpick inserted near the center comes out clean. Cool for 10 minutes before removing from pan to a wire rack to cool completely. YIELD: 1 LOAF (12 SLICES).

NUTRITION FACTS: 1 slice equals 176 calories, 6 g fat (1 g saturated fat), 50 mg cholesterol, 218 mg sodium, 26 g carbohydrate, 1 g fiber, 4 g protein. **DIABETIC EXCHANGES:** 1-1/2 starch, 1 fat.

roasted garlic and pepper pizza

roasted garlic and pepper pizza 🄻🄼

Years ago, I found the recipe for this appealing appetizer, lightened it and added some of our favorite ingredients. It can be prepared ahead of time and put in the oven as your guests arrive. We occasionally use it as an easy meal on busy weeknights.
—*Bonnie Matherly, Buckingham, Illinois*

1	large garlic bulb
1	teaspoon plus 2 tablespoons olive oil, *divided*
2	large sweet red peppers
1/2	cup sliced pimiento-stuffed olives
2	tablespoons red wine vinegar
1	teaspoon dried oregano
1/2	teaspoon dried basil
1/8	teaspoon white pepper
1	prebaked thin Italian bread shell crust (10 ounces)
4	slices sweet onion, separated into rings
3/4	cup crumbled feta cheese
1/3	cup shredded Parmesan cheese

Remove papery outer skin from the garlic (do not peel or separate cloves). Cut top off of garlic bulb. Brush with 1 teaspoon oil. Wrap the bulb in heavy-duty foil. Bake at 425° for 20-25 minutes or until softened. Cool for 10-15 minutes. Squeeze softened garlic onto a work surface; cut into thin slices.

Cut peppers in half; remove and discard seeds. Place cut side down on a baking sheet. Broil peppers 4 in. from the heat until skins blister, about 6 minutes. Immediately place peppers in a small bowl; cover and let stand for 15-20 minutes. Peel off and discard charred skins; cut peppers into thin strips.

In a small bowl, combine the olives, vinegar, oregano, basil, white pepper and remaining oil. Place crust on an ungreased 12-in. pizza pan; top with olive mixture, roasted garlic and peppers, onion and cheeses. Bake at 350° for 15-20 minutes or until cheese is melted. YIELD: 12 SLICES.

NUTRITION FACTS: 1 slice equals 138 calories, 7 g fat (2 g saturated fat), 10 mg cholesterol, 321 mg sodium, 14 g carbohydrate, 1 g fiber, 5 g protein. DIABETIC EXCHANGES: 1 starch, 1 fat.

moist corn bread 🄼

We like to indulge in this corn bread with a hot bowl of chili on cool fall evenings.
—*Christine Mazzarella, Brockport, New York*

1	egg, lightly beaten
1-1/2	cups fresh *or* frozen corn, thawed
1	can (8-3/4 ounces) cream-style corn
1	package (8-1/2 ounces) corn bread/ muffin mix
1	cup (8 ounces) fat-free plain yogurt
1/4	cup reduced-calorie stick margarine, melted

In a large bowl, combine all the ingredients. Pour into an 8-in. square baking dish coated with cooking spray.

Bake at 350° for 35-40 minutes or until edges are lightly browned and a toothpick inserted near the center comes out clean. Let stand for 10 minutes before cutting. YIELD: 9 SERVINGS.

NUTRITION FACTS: 1 piece equals 197 calories, 7 g fat (1 g saturated fat), 25 mg cholesterol, 452 mg sodium, 31 g carbohydrate, 3 g fiber, 5 g protein. DIABETIC EXCHANGES: 2 starch, 1 fat.

strawberry muffins 🄼

Recipes for good low-fat muffins are hard to find, so I was pleased to discover that these treats are moist and scrumptious. I make them often for brunches or parties, and people always comment on their fresh strawberry flavor.
—*Amanda Denton, Barre, Vermont*

1-3/4	cups all-purpose flour
3/4	cup sugar
1	teaspoon baking soda
1/4	teaspoon ground nutmeg
2	eggs, lightly beaten
1/2	cup fat-free plain yogurt
1/4	cup butter, melted and cooled
1	teaspoon vanilla extract
1-1/4	cups coarsely chopped fresh *or* frozen unsweetened strawberries

In a small bowl, combine first four ingredients. In another bowl, whisk the eggs, yogurt, butter and vanilla. Stir into the dry ingredients just until moistened. Fold in strawberries.

Fill muffin cups coated with cooking spray or lined with paper liners two-thirds full. Bake at 375° for 15-18 minutes or until a toothpick inserted near the center comes out clean. Cool for 5 minutes before removing from pan to a wire rack. Serve warm. YIELD: 1 DOZEN.

NUTRITION FACTS: 1 muffin equals 173 calories, 5 g fat (3 g saturated fat), 46 mg cholesterol, 163 mg sodium, 29 g carbohydrate, 1 g fiber, 4 g protein. DIABETIC EXCHANGES: 1 starch, 1 fruit, 1 fat.

herbed vegetable spiral bread ⓁⒻ Ⓜ️Ⓛ

This wonderful swirled bread is easy to put together...and while it's rising and baking, I make the rest of the meal. Pretty and flavorful, it's great for company or a special occason. It looks so fancy everyone thinks I buy this special golden loaf at a gourmet bakery!

—Deninelle Duncan, Markham, Ontario

1/2	cup shredded part-skim mozzarella cheese
1/2	cup canned Mexicorn, drained
1/4	cup grated Parmesan cheese
1/4	cup minced fresh parsley
2	garlic cloves, minced
1	teaspoon dried oregano
1/2	teaspoon dried basil
1/2	teaspoon ground cumin
1/4	teaspoon salt
1/8	to 1/4 teaspoon crushed red pepper flakes, optional
1	loaf (1 pound) frozen bread dough, thawed
1	tablespoon cornmeal
1	egg, lightly beaten

In a large bowl, combine the mozzarella, corn, Parmesan cheese, parsley, garlic and seasonings; set aside. On a lightly floured surface, roll dough into a 16-in. x 12-in. rectangle. Spread cheese mixture over dough to within 3/4 in. of edges.

Roll up jelly-roll style, starting with a long side; pinch seams and ends to seal. Sprinkle a large baking sheet with cornmeal. Place dough seam side down on baking sheet; tuck ends under. Cover and let rise in a warm place until doubled, about 35 minutes.

Brush with egg. Bake at 350° for 35-40 minutes or until golden brown and bread sounds hollow when tapped.

Cool for 20 minutes before slicing. Store leftovers in the refrigerator. YIELD: 16 SLICES.

NUTRITION FACTS: 1 slice equals 107 calories, 3 g fat (1 g saturated fat), 16 mg cholesterol, 280 mg sodium, 17 g carbohydrate, 1 g fiber, 5 g protein. DIABETIC EXCHANGES: 1 starch, 1/2 fat.

soy good snack mix Ⓜ️Ⓛ

A tasty takeoff on popular party munchies, this medley stirred up by our home economists blends nutritious roasted soybeans with crunchy cereal. Worcestershire sauce, vinegar and garlic powder combine for the zesty coating. You'll want to make extra batches of this mix, since handfuls disappear fast!

—Taste of Home Test Kitchen

5	cups Cheerios
5	cups Bran Chex
1/2	cup dry roasted soybeans
1/4	cup butter, melted
3	tablespoons Worcestershire sauce
1	tablespoon red wine vinegar
1/2	teaspoon garlic powder

In a large bowl, combine the cereals and soybeans. Combine the butter, Worcestershire sauce, vinegar and garlic powder; drizzle over cereal mixture and mix well.

Transfer to two ungreased 15-in. x 10-in. x 10-in. baking pans. Bake at 250° for 40-50 minutes, stirring every 15 minutes. Store in airtight containers.

YIELD: 8 SERVINGS.

NUTRITION FACTS: 1 cup equals 255 calories, 10 g fat (4 g saturated fat), 16 mg cholesterol, 513 mg sodium, 39 g carbohydrate, 5 g fiber, 9 g protein. DIABETIC EXCHANGES: 2 starch, 1 lean meat, 1 fat.

herbed vegetable spiral bread

Light COOKING TIP

Soybeans are made into many food products, and soybean products can be good sources for a variety of nutrients. When compared with many other legumes, soybeans have more protein and calcium, yet they're lower in complex carbohydrates. Common food products include soy milk, soy flour and tofu.

italian red pepper bruschetta (ML)

To make this easy appetizer, I halve a loaf of Italian bread, then top it with a blend of fresh basil, oregano, garlic and red peppers, tomatoes and cheeses. It's hard to eat just one slice!
—Josephine Devereaux Piro, Easton, Pennsylvania

1	loaf (1 pound) unsliced Italian bread
3	garlic cloves, minced, *divided*
3	tablespoons olive oil, *divided*
2	large sweet red peppers, chopped
1	medium onion, chopped
1-1/2	teaspoons Italian seasoning
2	tablespoons plus 1/4 cup coarsely chopped fresh basil, *divided*
2	tablespoons minced fresh parsley
1	tablespoon minced fresh oregano
6	plum tomatoes, sliced
3/4	cup shredded part-skim mozzarella cheese
3	slices reduced-fat provolone cheese, julienned
1/4	cup shredded Parmesan cheese

Cut bread in half lengthwise; place on a baking sheet. In a nonstick skillet, saute 2 garlic cloves in 2 tablespoons oil until tender. Brush over cut side of bread.

In the same skillet, saute the red peppers, onion, Italian seasoning and the remaining garlic in remaining oil until vegetables are tender; remove from heat. Add 2 tablespoons

italian red pepper bruschetta

basil, parsley and oregano; cool slightly. Place in a blender or food processor; cover and process until pureed. Spread over bread.

Top with tomato slices and cheeses. Sprinkle with remaining basil. Bake at 400° for 10-13 minutes or until cheese is melted and edges are golden brown. **YIELD: 12 SERVINGS.**

NUTRITION FACTS: 1 slice equals 190 calories, 7 g fat (2 g saturated fat), 8 mg cholesterol, 309 mg sodium, 24 g carbohydrate, 2 g fiber, 8 g protein. **DIABETIC EXCHANGES:** 1-1/2 starch, 1-1/2 fat.

honey whole wheat bread (ML)

You'll appreciate the hearty whole wheat goodness in this tender bread. The recipe calls for a combination of whole wheat and white flours to produce a loaf that tastes just like those Grandma used to make.
—Diane Kahnk, Tecumseh, Nebraska

1	cup water (70° to 80°)
1/4	cup canola oil
2	tablespoons honey
1	teaspoon salt
2	cups bread flour
1	cup whole wheat flour
1	package (1/4 ounce) active dry yeast (2-1/4 teaspoons)

In the bread machine pan, place all ingredients in order suggested by manufacturer. Select basic bread setting. Choose crust color and loaf size if available. Bake according to bread machine directions (check dough after 5 minutes of mixing; add 1 to 2 tablespoons of water or flour if needed). **YIELD: 1 LOAF (1-1/2 POUNDS, 16 SLICES).**

NUTRITION FACTS: 1 slice equals 127 calories, 146 mg sodium, 0 cholesterol, 20 g carbohydrate, 3 g protein, 4 g fat. **DIABETIC EXCHANGES:** 1 starch, 1 fat.

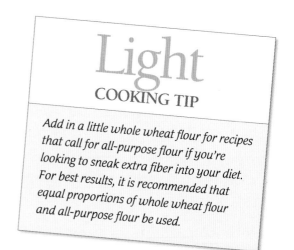

Light COOKING TIP

Add in a little whole wheat flour for recipes that call for all-purpose flour if you're looking to sneak extra fiber into your diet. For best results, it is recommended that equal proportions of whole wheat flour and all-purpose flour be used.

sweet 'n' spicy snack mix

sweet 'n' spicy snack mix ⓂⓁ

Cereal, cheesy snack crackers and mini pretzels are baked with a sprinkling of soy sauce, chili powder and barbecue seasoning. The mix is sure to spice up your next party or festive gathering.
—Taste of Home Test Kitchen

4	cups miniature pretzels
2-1/3	cups reduced-fat cheese-flavored baked snack crackers
2	cups Wheat Chex
3	tablespoons butter, melted
1	tablespoon reduced-sodium soy sauce
2	teaspoons chili powder
1	teaspoon barbecue seasoning
3	cups Corn Pops

In a large bowl, combine the pretzels, crackers and cereal. In a small bowl, combine the butter, soy sauce, chili powder and barbecue seasoning; pour over cereal mixture and toss to evenly coat.

Transfer to a 15-in. x 10-in. x 1-in. baking pan coated with cooking spray. Bake at 250° for 45 minutes, stirring every 15 minutes. Stir in Corn Pops. Store in airtight containers. **YIELD: 10 CUPS.**

NUTRITION FACTS: 3/4 cup equals 160 calories, 5 g fat (2 g saturated fat), 8 mg cholesterol, 484 mg sodium, 26 g carbohydrate, 1 g fiber, 3 g protein. **DIABETIC EXCHANGES:** 1-1/2 starch, 1 fat.

Editor's Note: If barbecue seasoning is not available in your grocery store, try Penzeys Spices. Call 1-800/741-7787 or visit www.penzeys.com.

tortellini appetizers ⓁⒸ

These cute kabobs will lend a little Italian flavor to any get-together. Cheese tortellini is marinated in salad dressing, then skewered on toothpicks along with stuffed olives, salami and cheese.
—Patricia Schmidt, Sterling Heights, Michigan

18	refrigerated cheese tortellini
1/4	cup fat-free Italian salad dressing
6	thin slices (4 ounces) reduced-fat provolone cheese
6	thin slices (2 ounces) Genoa salami
18	large pimiento-stuffed olives

Cook tortellini according to package directions; drain and rinse in cold water. In a resealable plastic bag, combine the tortellini and salad dressing. Seal bag and refrigerate for 4 hours.

Place a slice of cheese on each slice of salami; roll up tightly. Cut into thirds. Drain tortellini and discard dressing. For each appetizer, thread a tortellini, salami roll-up and olive on a toothpick. **YIELD: 1-1/2 DOZEN.**

NUTRITION FACTS: 2 appetizers equals 92 calories, 6 g fat (3 g saturated fat), 16 mg cholesterol, 453 mg sodium, 5 g carbohydrate, trace fiber, 7 g protein. **DIABETIC EXCHANGES:** 1 lean meat, 1 fat.

rosemary zucchini sticks ⓁⒻ ⓂⓁ

Our family loves zucchini, but fried zucchini has too much fat. So I baked these one day and everybody—even the grandchildren—thought they were great.
—Mrs. Betty Jackson, White Pine, Tennessee

2	medium zucchini, peeled
1	cup seasoned bread crumbs
1	tablespoon minced fresh rosemary *or* 1 teaspoon dried rosemary, crushed
1	egg
1	tablespoon water

Cut each zucchini in half widthwise, then cut each half lengthwise into quarters. In a shallow bowl, combine bread crumbs and rosemary. In another bowl, beat egg and water.

Dip zucchini in egg mixture, then coat with crumb mixture. Coat again in egg and crumbs. Arrange on a baking sheet coated with cooking spray. Bake at 375° for 20-25 minutes or until tender and golden, turning once. **YIELD: 4 SERVINGS.**

NUTRITION FACTS: 4 zucchini sticks equals 144 calories, 2 g fat (1 g saturated fat), 53 mg cholesterol, 814 mg sodium, 24 g carbohydrate, 2 g fiber, 7 g protein. **DIABETIC EXCHANGES:** 1-1/2 starch, 1/2 fat.

asparagus in puff pastry

asparagus in puff pastry ⓁⒸ ⓂⓁ

This is one of my famous appetizers. Fast and easy, the scrumptious bites are always a huge hit. I make and freeze batches of them during asparagus season for dinner parties throughout the year.

—Dianne Werdegar, Naperville, Illinois

2	cups water
24	fresh asparagus spears (about 1 pound), trimmed
1	package (8 ounces) reduced-fat cream cheese
1/2	teaspoon salt
1	package (17-1/4 ounces) frozen puff pastry dough, thawed
1/4	cup egg substitute

In a large nonstick skillet, bring water to a boil. Add asparagus; cover and cook for 3 minutes. Drain asparagus and immediately place in ice water; drain and pat dry. In a bowl, beat cream cheese and salt until smooth; set aside.

Unfold the dough on a lightly floured surface. Cut each sheet in half widthwise. For each rectangle, spread cream cheese mixture lengthwise over half of the dough to within 1/2 in. of edges. Arrange two rows of three asparagus spears lengthwise in a single layer over cream cheese.

Brush edges of dough with some of the egg substitute; fold dough over filling and press edges together to seal. Cover and refrigerate for 1 hour.

Cut widthwise into 1-1/4-in. pieces. Place 1 in. apart on a baking sheet coated with cooking spray. Brush with remaining egg substitute. Bake at 425° for 8-12 minutes or until golden. Serve warm. **YIELD: 28 SERVINGS.**

NUTRITION FACTS: 2 pieces equals 87 calories, 6 g fat (3 g saturated fat), 9 mg cholesterol, 156 mg sodium, 6 g carbohydrate, 1 g fiber, 3 g protein. **DIABETIC EXCHANGES:** 1 vegetable, 1/2 starch, 1/2 fat.

favorite buttermilk bread ⓂⓁ

This bread is an all-time favorite. Honey helps the crust bake up golden-brown, and wheat germ adds extra nutrition. The wonderful flavor will likely make it your family's standard for homemade bread, too.

—Michele Surgeon, Medford, Oregon

6	teaspoons active dry yeast
3/4	cup warm water (110° to 115°)
3	cups warm buttermilk (110° to 115°)
3/4	cup butter, melted and cooled
1/4	cup honey
3	teaspoons salt
1/2	teaspoon baking soda
3/4	cup toasted wheat germ
9	to 10 cups all-purpose flour

In a large bowl, dissolve yeast in warm water. Add the buttermilk, butter, honey, salt, baking soda, wheat germ and 4 cups flour. Beat until smooth. Gradually stir in enough remaining flour to make a soft dough.

Turn onto a heavily floured surface; knead until smooth and elastic, about 6-8 minutes. Place in a greased bowl, turning once to grease top. Cover and let rise in a warm place until doubled, about 1 hour.

Punch dough down. Turn onto a floured surface; divide into thirds. Divide each portion into thirds; shape each into a 12-in. rope. Braid three ropes; pinch ends to seal and tuck under. Place in a greased 9-in. x 5-in. loaf pan. Repeat with remaining dough. Cover and let rise until doubled, about 45 minutes.

Bake at 350° for 40-45 minutes or until golden brown. Remove from the pans to wire racks. **YIELD: 3 LOAVES (12 SLICES EACH).**

NUTRITION FACTS: 1 slice equals 183 calories, 4 g fat (3 g saturated fat), 11 mg cholesterol, 275 mg sodium, 31 g carbohydrate, 1 g fiber, 5 g protein. **DIABETIC EXCHANGES:** 2 starch, 1/2 fat.

Editor's Note: *Warmed buttermilk will appear curdled.*

favorite buttermilk bread

roasted vegetables with dip

roasted vegetables with dip (LF)(LC)(ML)

These colorful vegetables and zippy dip taste so good it never occurs to my clan that they're eating something nutritious and low in fat and calories.

—Melinda Sheridan, Pittsburg, Kansas

1/2	cup fat-free mayonnaise
1/4	cup fat-free sour cream
2	tablespoons salsa
1	garlic clove, minced
12	fresh mushrooms
1	medium sweet red pepper, cut into 1-1/2-inch pieces
1	medium green pepper, cut into 1-1/2-inch pieces
1	medium red onion, cut into wedges
1	medium yellow summer squash, cut into 1-1/2-inch pieces
1	tablespoon olive oil

In a small bowl, combine first four ingredients; refrigerate for 30 minutes or overnight.

In a large bowl, add mushrooms, peppers, onion and squash. Drizzle with the oil; toss to coat. Place in a single layer in an ungreased 15-in. x 10-in. x 1-in. baking pan.

Bake, uncovered, at 450° for 10 minutes or until crisp-tender. Serve with dip. **YIELD: 8 SERVINGS (1 CUP DIP).**

NUTRITION FACTS: 1 cup vegetables with 2 tablespoons dip equals 62 calories, 2 g fat (trace saturated fat), 3 mg cholesterol, 146 mg sodium, 9 g carbohydrate, 2 g fiber, 2 g protein. **DIABETIC EXCHANGES:** 2 vegetable, 1/2 fat.

sugar 'n' spice popcorn (LF)(LC)(LS)(ML)

Our family can't get enough of this light cinnamon-sweet popcorn. The baked kernels are wonderfully crunchy and coated just right. Try mixing some up to have on hand as an anytime nibble.

—Naomi Yoder, Leeseburg, Indiana

4	quarts air-popped popcorn
3	tablespoons butter
1/4	cup sugar
1	tablespoon water
1	teaspoon ground cinnamon
1/4	teaspoon salt

Place popcorn in a large roasting pan coated with cooking spray. In a small saucepan, melt butter over low heat. Add the sugar, water, cinnamon and salt; cook and stir over low heat until sugar is dissolved.

Pour over popcorn; toss to coat. Bake, uncovered, at 300° for 10-15 minutes. Serve immediately. **YIELD: 4 QUARTS.**

NUTRITION FACTS: 1 cup equals 62 calories, 2 g fat (1 g saturated fat), 6 mg cholesterol, 59 mg sodium, 9 g carbohydrate, 1 g fiber, 1 g protein. **DIABETIC EXCHANGES:** 1/2 starch, 1/2 fat.

lemon fruit dip (LC)(ML)

For a party, brunch buffet or healthy snack, fresh fruit with this sweet lemony dip can't be beat.

—Regina King, Watertown, Wisconsin

2	cups (16 ounces) reduced-fat sour cream
1	package (1 ounce) sugar-free instant vanilla pudding mix
1/4	cup fat-free milk
4	teaspoons lemon juice
1	teaspoon grated lemon peel

Assorted fresh fruit

In a bowl, whisk the sour cream, pudding mix, milk, lemon juice and peel until blended. Serve with fruit. **YIELD: 2 CUPS.**

NUTRITION FACTS: 1/3 cup equals 127 calories, 7 g fat (5 g saturated fat), 27 mg cholesterol, 255 mg sodium, 10 g carbohydrate, 0.55 g fiber, 6 g protein. **DIABETIC EXCHANGES:** 1 starch, 1 fat.

lemon fruit dip

spinach-stuffed bread (ML)

Appetizers are the highlight of parties at our home. Slices of this golden loaf swirled with spinach and cheese disappear in a hurry. They're a tasty accompaniment to most any meal, too.
—Terry Byrne, Warwick, New York

1	loaf (1 pound) frozen bread dough
1	medium onion, chopped
1	to 2 garlic cloves, minced
2	teaspoons olive oil
1	package (10 ounces) frozen chopped spinach, thawed and squeezed dry
2	cups (8 ounces) shredded reduced-fat cheddar *or* part-skim mozzarella

Thaw bread dough according to package directions; let rise until doubled. Meanwhile, in a skillet, saute onion and garlic in oil until tender. Stir in spinach.

On a lightly floured surface, roll the dough into a 14-in. x 10-in. rectangle. Spread the spinach mixture to within 1/2 in. of edges; sprinkle with cheese. Roll up jelly-roll style, starting with a long side; pinch seam to seal. Place seam side down on a baking sheet coated with cooking spray; tuck ends under.

Bake at 350° for 25-30 minutes or until golden brown. Remove from the pan to a wire rack; let stand for 10 minutes before slicing. Serve warm. **YIELD: 6 SERVINGS.**

NUTRITION FACTS: 2 slices equals 340 calories, 11 g fat (4 g saturated fat), 20 mg cholesterol, 687 mg sodium, 45 g carbohydrate, 4 g fiber, 21 g protein. **DIABETIC EXCHANGES:** 2 starch, 2 lean meat, 1-1/2 fat.

spinach-stuffed bread

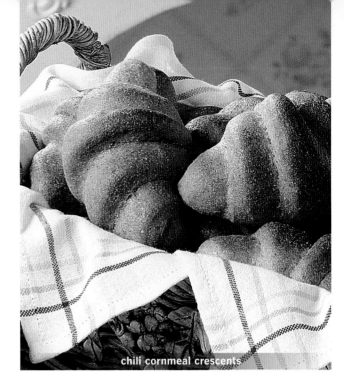
chili cornmeal crescents

chili cornmeal crescents (LF) (LS) (ML)

These unique rolls are tender, light and delicious, with a bit of chili tang. Use blue cornmeal for a fun change of pace.
—Marion Lowery, Medford, Oregon

1	package (1/4 ounce) active dry yeast
1-3/4	cups warm water (110° to 115°)
1-1/2	cups cornmeal
1/3	cup sugar
1	egg
2	tablespoons olive oil
1	tablespoon chili powder
1	teaspoon salt
4	to 4-1/2 cups all-purpose flour

In a large bowl, dissolve yeast in water. Add the cornmeal, sugar, egg, oil, chili powder, salt and 2 cups flour. Beat until smooth. Add enough remaining flour to form a soft dough.

Turn onto a floured surface; knead until smooth and elastic, about 6-8 minutes. Place in a greased bowl; turn once to grease top. Cover and let rise in a warm place until doubled, about 1 hour.

Punch the dough down; divide in half. Roll each portion into a 12-in. circle. Cut into 12 wedges. Roll up each wedge, starting with wide end. Place on greased baking sheet; curve into a crescent shape. Cover and let rise until doubled, about 30 minutes.

Bake at 375° for about 20 minutes or until browned. Cool on wire racks. **YIELD: 2 DOZEN.**

NUTRITION FACTS: 1 roll equals 129 calories, 2 g fat (0 saturated fat), 9 mg cholesterol, 106 mg sodium, 25 g carbohydrate, 0 fiber, 3 g protein. **DIABETIC EXCHANGES:** 1-1/2 starch, 1/2 fat.

western black bean dip (LF) (LC) (ML)

Indulge taste buds with this hearty bean dip full of flavors from the Southwest. After one taste, you'll know how good it is and wonder how it can be good for you, too!
—Pat Cassity, Boise, Idaho

- 1 can (15 ounces) black beans, rinsed and drained
- 1/2 cup plus 1 tablespoon chopped green onions, *divided*
- 1/2 cup plus 1 tablespoon chopped tomato, *divided*
- 1/2 cup salsa
- 3 garlic cloves, minced
- 1/2 teaspoon chili powder
- 1 teaspoon canola oil
- 1/4 cup shredded reduced-fat Mexican cheese blend, *divided*
- 1/4 cup minced fresh cilantro

Tortilla chips

In a large nonstick skillet, saute the beans, 1/2 cup onions, 1/2 cup tomato, salsa, garlic and chili powder in oil for 4-6 minutes or until heated through, gently mashing the beans while heating.

Remove from the heat. Stir in 3 tablespoons cheese and cilantro. Transfer to a serving dish; top with the remaining cheese, onions and tomato. Serve warm with chips. **YIELD: 1-1/2 CUPS.**

NUTRITION FACTS: 1/4 cup equals 92 calories, 2 g fat (1 g saturated fat), 3 mg cholesterol, 266 mg sodium, 13 g carbohydrate, 4 g fiber, 5 g protein. **DIABETIC EXCHANGES:** 1 starch, 1/2 fat.

healthy snack mix (ML)

If you're looking for a crunchy snack mix that's perfect for parties or to take along as a snack on-the-go, give this nutty whole-grain version a try.
—Cindy Giovanetti, Argyle, Texas

- 6 tablespoons egg substitute
- 3 tablespoons sesame seeds, toasted
- 2 tablespoons Worcestershire sauce
- 1 tablespoon seasoned salt
- 1 tablespoon fat-free cheese-flavored sprinkles
- 1-1/2 teaspoons onion powder
- 1-1/2 teaspoons garlic powder
- 1 teaspoon prepared mustard
- 1 package (16 ounces) Wheat Chex
- 1/3 cup *each* toasted almonds, salted cashews and dry-roasted peanuts

In a large bowl, whisk the first eight ingredients. Add the cereal and nuts; toss gently until coated. Spread onto two 15-in. x 10-in. x 1-in. baking pans coated with cooking spray. Bake at 250° for 20 minutes. Stir to break apart large pieces. Bake 30 minutes longer or until dried, stirring every 15 minutes. Spread on waxed paper-lined baking sheets to cool. Store in an airtight container. **YIELD: 18 SERVINGS.**

NUTRITION FACTS: 1/2 cup equals 147 calories, 5 g fat (1 g saturated fat), trace cholesterol, 536 mg sodium, 23 g carbohydrate, 4 g fiber, 5 g protein. **DIABETIC EXCHANGES:** 1-1/2 starch, 1 fat.

Editor's Note: *This recipe was tested with Molly McButter fat-free cheese-flavored sprinkles.*

turkey roll-ups

Whether served whole for lunch or cut into bite-size party starters, these light wraps are always a hit.
—Paula Alf, Cincinnati, Ohio

- 1 package (8 ounces) fat-free cream cheese
- 1/2 cup reduced-fat mayonnaise
- 1/4 teaspoon *each* dried basil and dried oregano
- 1/4 teaspoon dill weed
- 1/4 teaspoon garlic powder
- 10 flour tortillas (6 inches), room temperature
- 1 medium onion, chopped
- 10 slices deli turkey breast (1 ounce *each*)

Shredded lettuce

In a small bowl, combine the first six ingredients; beat until smooth. Spread over the tortillas. Sprinkle with onion; top with turkey and lettuce. Roll up tightly jelly-roll style; serve immediately. **YIELD: 10 SERVINGS.**

NUTRITION FACTS: 1 roll-up equals 259 calories, 9 g fat (2 g saturated fat), 17 mg cholesterol, 701 mg sodium, 33 g carbohydrate, 2 g fiber, 13 g protein. **DIABETIC EXCHANGES:** 2 starch, 1 lean meat, 1 fat.

Light COOKING TIP

Not all deli meats are created equal. "Sausage" style meats (bologna, pastrami, salami, etc.) have a higher fat content than leaner meats such as chicken or turkey breast. If possible, select organic deli meats, or at least check to be sure they are free of MSG.

dill bread

dill bread (LF) (ML)

This golden-brown loaf is moist and flavorful. Dill weed gives each wedge an herbed zest, making it a nice complement to most any meal. The best part is that this easy yeast bread requires no kneading, so preparation is a snap!
—Corky Huffsmith, Salem, Oregon

- 1 package (1/4 ounce) active dry yeast
- 1/4 cup warm water (110° to 115°)
- 1 cup (8 ounces) 2% cottage cheese
- 1/4 cup snipped fresh dill *or* 4 teaspoons dill weed
- 1 tablespoon butter, melted
- 1-1/2 teaspoons salt
- 1 teaspoon sugar
- 1 teaspoon dill seed
- 1 egg, lightly beaten
- 2-1/4 to 2-3/4 cups all-purpose flour

In a large bowl, dissolve yeast in warm water. In a small saucepan, heat cottage cheese to 110°-115°; add to yeast mixture. Add the fresh dill, butter, salt, sugar, dill seed, egg and 1 cup flour; beat until smooth. Stir in enough remaining flour to form a soft dough. Do not knead. Cover and let rise in a warm place until doubled, about 1 hour.

Punch dough down. Turn onto a lightly floured surface; shape into a 6-in. circle. Transfer to a 9-in. round baking pan coated with cooking spray. Cover and let rise until doubled, about 45 minutes.

Bake at 350° for 35-40 minutes or until bread sounds hollow when tapped. Remove from pan to a wire rack to cool. Cut into wedges before serving. **YIELD: 12 SERVINGS.**

NUTRITION FACTS: 1 piece equals 118 calories, 2 g fat (1 g saturated fat), 22 mg cholesterol, 385 mg sodium, 19 g carbohydrate, 1 g fiber, 6 g protein. **DIABETIC EXCHANGES:** 1 starch, 1/2 fat.

five-fruit salsa (ML)

Scoop this chunky, fresh-tasting salsa onto a cinnamon tortilla chip and you just won't be able to resist going back for more.
—Catherine Dawe, Kent, Ohio

- 2 cups chopped fresh cantaloupe
- 6 green onions, chopped
- 3 kiwifruit, peeled and finely chopped
- 1 medium navel orange, peeled and finely chopped
- 1 medium sweet yellow pepper, chopped
- 1 medium sweet red pepper, chopped
- 2 jalapeno peppers, seeded and chopped
- 1 can (8 ounces) crushed unsweetened pineapple, drained

CINNAMON TORTILLA CHIPS:

- 10 flour tortillas (8 inches)
- 1/4 cup butter, melted
- 1/3 cup sugar
- 2 teaspoons ground cinnamon
- 1 cup finely chopped fresh strawberries

In a large bowl, combine the cantaloupe, onions, kiwi, orange, peppers and pineapple. Cover and refrigerate for 8 hours or overnight.

For chips, brush the tortillas with butter; cut into eight wedges. Combine sugar and cinnamon; sprinkle over the tortillas. Place on ungreased baking sheets. Bake at 350° for 10-14 minutes or just until crisp.

Just before serving, drain salsa if desired. Stir in strawberries. Serve fruit salsa with cinnamon chips. **YIELD: 8 CUPS.**

NUTRITION FACTS: 1/2 cup salsa with 5 chips equals 150 calories, 5 g fat (2 g saturated fat), 8 mg cholesterol, 189 mg sodium, 29 g carbohydrate, 2 g fiber, 4 g protein. **DIABETIC EXCHANGES:** 2 fruit, 1 fat.

Editor's Note: *When cutting hot peppers, disposable gloves are recommended. Avoid touching your face.*

five-fruit salsa

refrigerator rolls

refrigerator rolls (LF)(LS)(ML)

These rolls are crusty on the outside and sweet and tender on the inside. The easy-to-handle dough rises in the refrigerator overnight for added convenience.
—*Martha Sue Stroud, Clarksville, Texas*

1	package (1/4 ounce) active dry yeast
2-1/2	cups warm water (110° to 115°), *divided*
1/2	cup shortening
1/2	cup sugar
1	egg
1-1/2	teaspoons salt
7	cups all-purpose flour

In a small bowl, dissolve yeast in 1/2 cup water; set aside.

In a large bowl, cream shortening and sugar. Add egg, salt, 4 cups flour, yeast mixture and remaining water; beat until smooth. Add enough remaining water; beat until smooth. Add enough remaining flour to form a soft dough.

Turn onto a floured surface and knead until smooth and elastic, about 6-8 minutes. Place in a greased bowl, turning once to grease top. Cover and refrigerate for 8 hours or overnight.

Punch dough down and divide into thirds; shape each portion into 12 rolls in desired shape. Place on greased baking sheets. Cover and let rise in a warm place until doubled, about 1 hour.

Bake at 400° for 12-14 minutes or until lightly browned. **YIELD: 3 DOZEN.**

NUTRITION FACTS: 1 roll (prepared with egg substitute equivalent to one egg) equals 126 calories, 3 g fat (0 saturated fat), trace cholesterol, 101 mg sodium, 21 g carbohydrate, 0 fiber, 3 g protein. **DIABETIC EXCHANGES:** 1-1/2 starch, 1/2 fat.

vegetable bites (ML)

You save time by using a tube of refrigerated crescent rolls as the crust for these snacks. It's also easy to double the recipe when you need to prepare a big batch for a crowd.
—*Corey Henderson, Calgary, Alberta*

1	tube (4 ounces) refrigerated crescent rolls
4	ounces cream cheese, softened
1	tablespoon mayonnaise
1-1/2	teaspoons ranch salad dressing mix
1/2	cup finely chopped fresh broccoli
1/2	cup finely chopped fresh cauliflower
3	tablespoons chopped sweet red pepper
3	tablespoons chopped green pepper

Unroll the crescent dough onto a baking sheet forming a 14-in. x 3-1/2-in. rectangle; seal perforations. Bake dough at 375° for 7-9 minutes or until golden brown. Cool completely on a wire rack. In a large bowl, beat the cream cheese, mayonnaise and salad dressing mix until blended. Spread evenly over crust. Sprinkle with vegetables; gently press down. Cover with plastic wrap. Chill until serving. Cut into squares. **YIELD: 4 SERVINGS.**

NUTRITION FACTS: 1 serving (prepared with reduced-fat cream cheese and fat-free mayonnaise) equals 191 calories, 11 g fat (5 g saturated fat), 16 mg cholesterol, 403 mg sodium, 16 g carbohydrate, 1 g fiber, 6 g protein. **DIABETIC EXCHANGES:** 2 fat, 1 starch.

vegetable bites

light guacamole (LC) (ML)

Feel guilty dipping into guacamole? This low-fat version is a yummy alternative. It has chunky bits of tomato and is well seasoned with jalapeno peppers, cumin and cilantro.

—Marlene Tokarski, Mesa, Arizona

2	large ripe avocados, peeled, *divided*
1	cup (8 ounces) fat-free sour cream
1/4	cup chopped onion
3	jalapeno peppers, seeded and chopped
6	tablespoons minced fresh cilantro
4	teaspoons lemon juice
1/2	teaspoon salt
1/2	teaspoon ground cumin
1/8	teaspoon pepper
1	large tomato, seeded and chopped

Tortilla chips *or* fresh vegetables

In a food processor, combine one avocado, sour cream, onion, jalapenos, cilantro, lemon juice, salt, cumin and pepper; cover and process until smooth.

In a small bowl, mash the remaining avocado with a fork. Stir in the pureed avocado mixture. Gently fold in tomato. Serve with tortilla chips or vegetables. **YIELD: 3 CUPS.**

NUTRITION FACTS: 1/4 cup equals 79 calories, 5 g fat (1 g saturated fat), 2 mg cholesterol, 119 mg sodium, 7 g carbohydrate, 2 g fiber, 2 g protein. **DIABETIC EXCHANGES:** 1 vegetable, 1 fat.

Editor's Note: *When cutting hot peppers, disposable gloves are recommended. Avoid touching your face.*

light guacamole

Light COOKING TIP

It's easy to remove the seed, or pit, from an avocado. Simply wash the avocado and cut in half lengthwise, cutting around the seed. Twist halves in opposite directions to separate. Slip a tablespoon under the seed to loosen it. Loosen the avocado flesh from the skin with a large spoon and scoop out. Save the seed to add to the guacamole. If the dish is covered, the dip retains its fresh, garden-green color.

---

cranberry-apple bread (ML)

Don't wait until the holiday season to bake these lovely little loaves. This quick bread is wonderful anytime. With its sweet-tart mix of apples and cranberries, the loaves store well in the freezer, too.

—Patricia Kile, Greentown, Pennsylvania

2-1/3	cups reduced-fat biscuit/baking mix
3/4	cup sugar
5	egg whites
1/2	cup reduced-fat sour cream
1/4	cup fat-free milk
1/4	cup canola oil
1	teaspoon grated orange peel
1	cup chopped peeled apple
3/4	cup fresh *or* frozen cranberries, chopped
1/2	cup confectioners' sugar
2	to 3 teaspoons orange juice

In a large bowl, combine biscuit mix and sugar. In another bowl, whisk the egg whites, sour cream, milk, oil and orange peel. Stir into dry ingredients just until moistened. Fold in apple and cranberries.

Pour into three 5-3/4-in. x 3-in. x 2-in. loaf pans coated with cooking spray. Bake at 375° for 35-40 minutes or until a toothpick inserted near the center comes out clean. Cool for 10 minutes before removing from pans to wire racks.

In a small bowl, combine confectioners' sugar and enough orange juice to achieve a drizzling consistency; drizzle over cooled loaves. **YIELD: 3 LOAVES (8 SLICES EACH).**

NUTRITION FACTS: 1 slice equals 113 calories, 4 g fat (1 g saturated fat), 2 mg cholesterol, 156 mg sodium, 18 g carbohydrate, trace fiber, 2 g protein. **DIABETIC EXCHANGES:** 1 starch, 1/2 fat.

cheesy artichoke mini tarts ⓜ

Good-for-you things come in tasty little packages when you follow this recipe. Wonton wrappers form the crisp cups that hold the cheddary artichoke filling in these cute appetizers.
—Barbara Nowakowski, North Tonawanda, New York

- 36 wonton wrappers
- 1 package (8 ounces) reduced-fat cream cheese
- 1 cup (4 ounces) shredded reduced-fat cheddar cheese
- 1 tablespoon Dijon mustard
- 1/4 to 1/2 teaspoon cayenne pepper
- 1 can (14 ounces) water-packed artichoke hearts, rinsed, drained and chopped
- 1/4 cup chopped sweet red pepper

Fresh dill *or* tarragon sprigs, optional

Gently press wonton wrappers into miniature muffins cups coated with cooking spray, allowing edges to extend above cups. Spritz edges with cooking spray.

In a large bowl, combine the cream cheese, cheddar cheese, mustard and cayenne until blended. Stir in artichokes and red pepper. Spoon into wonton cups.

Bake at 350° for 18-20 minutes or until cheese mixture is set and wontons are lightly browned. Garnish with dill or tarragon if desired. **YIELD: 3 DOZEN.**

NUTRITION FACTS: 3 filled wontons equals 157 calories, 5 g fat (3 g saturated fat), 18 mg cholesterol, 483 mg sodium, 19 g carbohydrate, 2 g fiber, 8 g protein. **DIABETIC EXCHANGES:** 1 starch, 1 vegetable, 1 fat.

vegetable focaccia ⓜ

This popular recipe began as herb focaccia but gradually came to include our favorite vegetables. There's no cheese because my husband can't have dairy products. But some people who try it think it has cheese anyway!
—Michele Fairchok, Grove City, Ohio

- 2 to 2-1/4 cups bread flour
- 1 package (1/4 ounce) quick-rise yeast
- 1 teaspoon salt
- 1 cup warm water (120° to 130°)
- 1 tablespoon olive oil

TOPPING:
- 3 plum tomatoes, chopped
- 5 medium fresh mushrooms, sliced
- 1/2 cup chopped green pepper
- 1/2 cup sliced ripe olives
- 1/4 cup chopped onion
- 3 tablespoons olive oil
- 2 teaspoons red wine vinegar
- 3/4 teaspoon salt
- 1/4 teaspoon garlic powder
- 1/4 teaspoon dried oregano
- 1/4 teaspoon pepper
- 2 teaspoons cornmeal

In a large bowl, combine 2 cups flour, yeast and salt. Add water and oil; beat until smooth. Stir in enough remaining flour to form a soft dough.

Turn onto a floured surface; knead until smooth and elastic, about 4 minutes. Cover and let rest for 15 minutes. Meanwhile, in a bowl, combine the tomatoes, mushrooms, green pepper, olives, onion, oil, vinegar and seasonings.

Coat a 15-in. x 10-in. x 1-in. baking pan with cooking spray; sprinkle with cornmeal. Press dough into pan. Prick dough generously with a fork.

Bake at 475° for 5 minutes or until lightly browned. Cover with vegetable mixture. Bake 8-10 minutes longer or until edges of crust are golden brown. **YIELD: 12 SERVINGS.**

NUTRITIONAL FACTS: 1 piece equals 121 calories, 5 g fat (1 g saturated fat), 0 cholesterol, 376 mg sodium, 17 g carbohydrate, 1 g fiber, 3 g protein. **DIABETIC EXCHANGES:** 1 starch, 1 fat.

vegetable focaccia

soups, salads & sides

grilled corn
pasta salad
page 59

roasted potato salad

roasted potato salad (LF) (ML)

I pack this delicious potato salad in a cooler to dish up cold at picnics or transfer it to a slow cooker to serve warm for church potlucks.

—Terri Adams, Kansas City, Kansas

6	cups water	2	green onions, sliced
1/2	pound fresh green beans, cut into 1-1/2-inch pieces	1/4	cup balsamic vinegar
1	large whole garlic bulb	2	tablespoons olive oil
2	pounds small red potatoes, quartered	2	teaspoons sugar
		1	teaspoon minced fresh rosemary *or* 1/4 teaspoon dried rosemary, crushed
1/4	cup chicken broth		
2	medium sweet red peppers, cut into large chunks	1/2	teaspoon salt

In a large saucepan, bring 6 cups water to a boil. Add beans; bring to a boil. Cover and cook for 3 minutes. Drain and immediately place beans in ice water; drain and pat dry.

Remove papery outer skin from garlic (do not peel or separate cloves). Cut top off garlic bulb. Place cut side up in a greased 15-in. x 10-in. x 1-in. baking pan. Add potatoes; drizzle with broth. Bake, uncovered, at 400° for 30-40 minutes or until garlic is softened.

Remove garlic; set aside. Add the red peppers, onions and reserved beans to the pan. Bake 30-35 minutes longer or until tender. Cool for 10-15 minutes.

Squeeze softened garlic into a large bowl. Stir in the vinegar, oil, sugar, rosemary and salt. Add vegetables; toss to coat. Serve warm or cold. **YIELD: 9 SERVINGS.**

NUTRITION FACTS: 3/4 cup equals 124 calories, 3 g fat (trace saturated fat), 0 cholesterol, 167 mg sodium, 22 g carbohydrate, 3 g fiber, 3 g protein. **DIABETIC EXCHANGES:** 1 starch, 1 vegetable, 1/2 fat.

Light COOKING TIP

Ditch potato salads weighed down in mayo and opt for those that feature a clean, fresh taste from herbs and other seasonings. This recipe calls for rosemary, which has an intense, earthy flavor. It's strong, so use it sparingly.

vegetarian chili

vegetarian chili ML

My husband and I try to have at least one vegetarian meal each week, and this is one of our favorites. The recipe makes a large pot of chili that's loaded with protein. Once the chopping is done, it's quick to cook.
—Marilyn Barilleaux, Bothell, Washington

4	medium zucchini, chopped
2	medium onions, chopped
1	medium green pepper, chopped
1	medium sweet red pepper, chopped
4	garlic cloves, minced
1/4	cup olive oil
2	cans (28 ounces *each*) Italian stewed tomatoes, cut up
1	can (15 ounces) tomato sauce
1	can (15 ounces) pinto beans, rinsed and drained
1	can (15 ounces) black beans, rinsed and drained
1	jalapeno pepper, seeded and chopped
1/4	cup *each* minced fresh cilantro and parsley
2	tablespoons chili powder
1	tablespoon sugar
1	teaspoon salt
1	teaspoon ground cumin

In a Dutch oven, saute the zucchini, onions, peppers and garlic in oil until tender. Stir in the tomatoes, tomato sauce, beans, jalapeno and seasonings. Bring to a boil over medium heat. Reduce heat; cover and simmer for 30 minutes, stirring occasionally. **YIELD: 16 SERVINGS.**

NUTRITION FACTS: 1 cup equals 131 calories, 4 g fat (trace saturated fat), 0 cholesterol, 622 mg sodium, 18 g carbohydrate, 6 g fiber, 5 g protein. **DIABETIC EXCHANGES:** 1 starch, 1 vegetable, 1 fat.

Editor's Note: When cutting hot peppers, disposable gloves are recommended. Avoid touching your face.

sweet-sour zucchini salad LC LS ML

This make-ahead mixture can be served as a condiment or a salad. The flavorful marinade is also nice with cucumbers.
—Jan Koppri, Mancos, Colorado

1/2	cup cider vinegar
4-1/2	teaspoons dried minced onion
7	small zucchini, thinly sliced
1/2	cup chopped celery
1/4	cup chopped green pepper
1/4	cup chopped sweet red pepper

DRESSING:

3/4	cup sugar
2/3	cup cider vinegar
1/3	cup canola oil
1	teaspoon salt, optional
1	teaspoon pepper

In a large bowl, combine the vinegar and onion. Add the zucchini, celery and peppers.

In a jar with a tight-fitting lid, combine the dressing ingredients; shake well. Pour over the vegetables and stir gently. Cover and refrigerate for 8 hours or overnight. Serve with a slotted spoon. **YIELD: 10 SERVINGS.**

NUTRITION FACTS: 3/4-cup serving (prepared with artificial sweetener equivalent to 3/4 cup sugar and without salt) equals 113 calories, 7 g fat (0 saturated fat), 0 cholesterol, 9 mg sodium, 10 g carbohydrate, 0 fiber, 1 g protein. **DIABETIC EXCHANGES:** 2 vegetable, 1-1/2 fat.

sweet-sour zucchini salad

roasted chicken noodle soup

roasted chicken noodle soup ⓛⒻ

When the weather turns chilly, stock your soup pot with this warmer-upper. The creamy, nicely seasoned broth is chock-full of tender chicken, potatoes, carrots and celery. There's old-fashioned goodness in every spoonful.
—*Julee Wallberg, Salt Lake City, Utah*

1	cup chopped onion
1	cup chopped carrots
1	cup chopped celery
1	garlic clove, minced
2	teaspoons olive oil
1/4	cup all-purpose flour
1/2	teaspoon dried oregano
1/4	teaspoon dried thyme
1/4	teaspoon poultry seasoning
6	cups reduced-sodium chicken broth
4	cups cubed peeled potatoes
1	teaspoon salt
2	cups cubed cooked chicken breast
2	cups uncooked yolk-free wide noodles
1	cup fat-free evaporated milk

In a stockpot, saute the onion, carrots, celery and garlic in oil for 5 minutes or until tender. Stir in the flour, oregano, thyme and poultry seasoning until blended; saute 1 minute longer.

Gradually add the broth, potatoes and salt; bring to a boil. Reduce heat; cover and simmer for 15-20 minutes or until potatoes are tender.

Stir in chicken and noodles; simmer for 10 minutes or until noodles are tender. Reduce heat. Stir in milk; heat through (do not boil). **YIELD: 8 SERVINGS.**

NUTRITION FACTS: 1-1/2 cups equals 235 calories, 3 g fat (1 g saturated fat), 31 mg cholesterol, 851 mg sodium, 33 g carbohydrate, 3 g fiber, 20 g protein. **DIABETIC EXCHANGES:** 2 very lean meat, 1-1/2 starch, 1 vegetable, 1/2 fat.

italian zucchini boats Ⓜ️Ⓛ

The tantalizing aroma of this savory side dish baking in the oven is sure to whet your appetite. Mom scoops the pulp out of zucchini halves and mixes it with tomato, Parmesan cheese, bread crumbs and parsley.
—*Concetta Maranto Skenfield, Bakersfield, California*

6	medium zucchini
2	cups dry bread crumbs
2	eggs, lightly beaten
1	large tomato, diced
1/3	cup grated Parmesan cheese
1/4	cup minced fresh parsley
2	garlic cloves, minced
1/2	cup chicken broth
1/2	teaspoon salt
1/8	teaspoon pepper
2	tablespoons butter, melted

Cut zucchini in half lengthwise. Scoop out pulp, leaving a 3/8-in. shell. Reserve pulp. Cook shells in salted water for 2 minutes. Remove and drain. Set aside. Chop zucchini pulp. Transfer to a large bowl; add the bread crumbs, eggs, tomato, Parmesan cheese, parsley and garlic. Stir in broth, salt and pepper. Fill zucchini shells.

Place in a greased 13-in. x 9-in. baking dish. Drizzle with butter. Bake, uncovered, at 350° for 20 minutes or until golden brown. **YIELD: 6 SERVINGS.**

NUTRITION FACTS: 2 stuffed zucchini halves equals 260 calories, 9 g fat (4 g saturated fat), 85 mg cholesterol, 741 mg sodium, 34 g carbohydrate, 4 g fiber, 11 g protein. **DIABETIC EXCHANGES:** 2 starch, 1-1/2 fat, 1 vegetable.

italian zucchini boats

herbed mashed potatoes (ML)

A touch of rosemary, garlic and lemon peel add wonderful flavor to these rich mashed potatoes, making it special enough for guests. One bite and you'll see that these potatoes are anything but ordinary.

—Sandra Pichon, Slidell, Louisiana

4	large potatoes, peeled and cubed
1/3	cup chopped onion
1	garlic clove, minced
1	tablespoon butter
3/4	cup sour cream
1	teaspoon dill weed
1/4	to 1 teaspoon salt
1/2	teaspoon minced fresh rosemary
1/2	teaspoon grated lemon peel
1/4	teaspoon crushed red pepper flakes, optional

Paprika, optional

Place potatoes in a saucepan and cover with water; cover and bring to a boil over medium-high heat. Cook for 15-20 minutes or until tender. Meanwhile, in a skillet, saute onion and garlic in butter until tender.

Drain and mash potatoes; add the onion mixture, sour cream, dill, salt, rosemary, lemon peel and red pepper flakes if desired.

Spoon into a greased 1-1/2-qt. baking dish. Sprinkle with paprika if desired. Cover and bake at 350° for 25 minutes or until heated through. **YIELD: 6 SERVINGS.**

NUTRITION FACTS: 3/4 cup equals 160 calories, 5 g fat (3 g saturated fat), 15 mg cholesterol, 145 mg sodium, 25 g carbohydrate, 2 g fiber, 5 g protein. **DIABETIC EXCHANGES:** 1-1/2 starch, 1 fat.

herbed mashed potatoes

dressed-up broccoli (ML)

You need only four ingredients to turn ordinary broccoli into a dressed-up side dish. The garlic in the broiled crumb topping really comes through. Plus, you know you're getting an extra dose of calcium and vitamin C for the day.

—Bryan Forster, Clayton, Ontario

3-1/2	cups broccoli florets
3	tablespoons dry bread crumbs
2	tablespoons grated Parmesan cheese
1	tablespoon butter, melted
2	to 3 garlic cloves, minced

Place the broccoli and a small amount of water in a microwave- and broiler-safe 1-1/2-qt. dish. Cover dish and microwave on high until crisp-tender, about 4-1/2 minutes; drain. Combine remaining ingredients; sprinkle over broccoli. Broil for 3-4 minutes or until lightly browned. **YIELD: 4 SERVINGS.**

NUTRITION FACTS: 1/2 cup equals 50 calories, 1 g fat (1 g saturated fat), 2 mg cholesterol, 92 mg sodium, 7 g carbohydrate, 2 g fiber, 4 g protein. **DIABETIC EXCHANGES:** 1 vegetable, 1/2 fat.

Editor's Note: This recipe was tested in a 1,100-watt microwave.

fruit 'n' cheese salad (ML)

Sweet dressing, tart grapefruit sections, toasted walnuts and pungent blue cheese come together in this out-of-the-ordinary salad. The recipe showcases one of the citrus fruits my brother, Ed, and I grow in Indian River County.

—Fred Peterson, Vero Beach, Florida

8	to 10 cups torn salad greens
3	medium grapefruit, peeled and sectioned
1	cup halved seedless red grapes
3/4	cup crumbled blue cheese
1/2	cup thinly sliced red onion
1/4	cup chopped walnuts, toasted, optional
1	cup cider vinegar
2	tablespoons olive oil
2	tablespoons honey
1	tablespoon Dijon mustard
1/4	teaspoon salt, optional

In a large bowl, combine the salad greens, fruit, cheese, onion and nuts if desired. In a small bowl, whisk vinegar, oil, honey, mustard and salt if desired. Pour over salad; toss to coat. **YIELD: 8-10 SERVINGS.**

NUTRITION FACTS: 126 calories, 6 g fat, 8 mg cholesterol, 195 mg sodium, 16 g carbohydrate, 4 g protein. **DIABETIC EXCHANGES:** 1 fruit, 1 fat, 1/2 meat.

bacon 'n' veggie pasta

bacon 'n' veggie pasta ⊕

When the weather turns chilly, our daughter, who is an inventive cook, transforms her favorite cold pasta salad into this warm, hearty pasta. I love recipes like this one that bring compliments and don't keep me in the kitchen too long.
—Muriel Hollenbeck, Sedalia, Colorado

2	cans (14-1/2 ounces *each*) stewed tomatoes
2	cups fresh broccoli florets
2	medium carrots, thinly sliced
1/2	teaspoon salt
1/2	teaspoon Italian seasoning
1/2	teaspoon dried oregano
1/4	teaspoon dried basil
4	bacon strips, diced
1/2	pound fresh mushrooms, sliced
1/3	cup chopped green pepper
1/4	cup chopped onion
2	garlic cloves, minced
16	ounces uncooked medium shell pasta
1/4	cup shredded Parmesan cheese

In a large saucepan, combine the first seven ingredients. Bring to a boil. Reduce heat; cover and simmer for 25-30 minutes or until broccoli and carrots are tender.

In a large skillet, cook bacon over medium heat until crisp. Remove to paper towels; drain, reserving 1 tablespoon drippings. In the drippings, saute the mushrooms, green pepper, onion and garlic until tender; add to the tomato mixture and heat through.

Meanwhile, cook the pasta according to the package directions. Drain and place in a serving bowl; top with vegetable mixture. Sprinkle with bacon and Parmesan cheese. YIELD: 13 SERVINGS.

NUTRITION FACTS: 3/4 cup equals 205 calories, 3 g fat (1 g saturated fat), 4 mg cholesterol, 289 mg sodium, 36 g carbohydrate, 3 g fiber, 8 g protein. **DIABETIC EXCHANGES:** 2 starch, 1 vegetable, 1/2 fat.

colorful corn ⓁⒸ ⓁⓈ ⓂⓁ

I've been serving this lovely creamed dish for many years. It starts with convenient frozen corn and gets garden-fresh taste from green pepper, tomato and onion.
—Donna Gonda, North Canton, Ohio

1	package (16 ounces) frozen corn
1/4	cup butter, melted
1	small onion, thinly sliced
1/2	cup julienned green pepper
1/2	to 1 teaspoon salt, optional
1/4	cup milk
2	medium tomatoes, chopped

In a large saucepan, cook corn according to the package directions; drain. Add the butter, onion, green pepper and salt if desired. Cook over low heat for 3-5 minutes or until vegetables are heated through. Add milk; bring to a boil.

Reduce heat; simmer for 2 minutes or until heated through. Remove from the heat; stir in tomatoes. YIELD: 8 SERVINGS.

NUTRITION FACTS: 3/4 cup (prepared with fat-free milk and without salt) equals 114 calories, 6 g fat (4 g saturated fat), 15 mg cholesterol, 48 mg sodium, 15 g carbohydrate, 2 g fiber, 3 g protein. **DIABETIC EXCHANGES:** 1-1/2 fat, 1 starch, 1 vegetable.

colorful corn

Light
COOKING TIP

Indulge taste buds and boost nutritional intake by adding leftover vegetables to soups, stews or chili. Or, add them to salads or whole grain pasta dishes.

west coast potato salad

west coast potato salad (LF) (LC) (LS) (ML)

This potato salad incorporates tender asparagus and the tongue-tingling tang of herbs and lemon juice. Here in the San Francisco Bay area, which is close to the California's primary asparagus-growing region, we look forward to spring when we can harvest it to use in dishes like this.
—*Phyllis Lee Ciardo, Albany, California*

1-1/2	pounds medium red potatoes, cooked and cubed
4	tablespoons lemon juice, *divided*
2	tablespoons canola oil
2	tablespoons minced fresh parsley
1/2	teaspoon salt, optional
1/4	teaspoon pepper
3/4	cup thinly sliced celery
1/4	cup chopped green onions
1	pound fresh asparagus, cut into 3/4-inch pieces
1/2	cup sour cream
2	tablespoons Dijon mustard
1	teaspoon dried thyme
1	teaspoon dried tarragon

Place potatoes in a large bowl and set aside. In a jar with tight-fitting lid, combine 3 tablespoons lemon juice, oil, parsley, salt if desired and pepper; shake well. Pour over potatoes and toss gently. Add celery and onions; set aside.

In a large saucepan, bring 1/2 in. of water to a boil. Add the asparagus; cover and cook for 3 minutes. Drain and immediately place asparagus in ice water. Drain and pat dry. Add to potato mixture.

In a small bowl, combine the sour cream, mustard, thyme, tarragon and remaining lemon juice; gently fold into salad. Chill until serving. YIELD: 12 SERVINGS.

NUTRITION FACTS: 1/2-cup serving (prepared with fat-free sour cream and without salt) equals 80 calories, 3 g fat (0 saturated fat), 1 mg cholesterol, 83 mg sodium, 11 g carbohydrate, 0 fiber, 3 g protein. DIABETIC EXCHANGES: 1 vegetable, 1/2 starch, 1/2 fat.

pasta pizza soup

A steaming bowl of this soup hits the spot on a cold rainy or snowy day, which we have in abundance here in Alaska. Oregano adds fast flavor to the pleasant combination of tender vegetables, pasta spirals and ground beef.
—*Linda Fox, Soldotna, Alaska*

1	pound ground beef
4	ounces sliced fresh mushrooms
1	medium onion, chopped
1	celery rib, thinly sliced
1	garlic clove, minced
4	cups water
1	can (14-1/2 ounces) Italian diced tomatoes, undrained
2	medium carrots, sliced
4	teaspoons beef bouillon granules
1	bay leaf
1-1/2	teaspoons dried oregano
1-1/2	cups cooked tricolor spiral pasta

In a large saucepan over medium heat, cook the beef, mushrooms, onion, celery and garlic until meat is no longer pink; drain.

Stir in the water, tomatoes, carrots, bouillon, bay leaf and oregano. Bring to a boil. Reduce the heat; cover and simmer for 20-25 minutes or until carrots are tender. Stir in pasta; heat through. Discard bay leaf. YIELD: 8 SERVINGS (ABOUT 2 QUARTS).

NUTRITION FACTS: 1 serving (prepared with low-sodium bouillon) equals 168 calories, 5 g fat (2 g saturated fat), 28 mg cholesterol, 401 mg sodium, 17 g carbohydrate, 2 g fiber, 13 g protein. DIABETIC EXCHANGES: 2 vegetable, 1 lean meat, 1/2 starch, 1/2 fat.

pasta pizza soup

orange cucumber tossed salad

orange cucumber tossed salad ⓁⒸ Ⓜ

This recipe has been a family favorite for as long as I can remember. Everyone loves the fresh flavor of oranges and sliced cucumber spread over leafy greens. Often, I'll double the ingredients for dressing so I have some on hand for the next time I make this delightful salad.
—*Betty Tobias, Nashua, New Hampshire*

2	medium navel oranges, peeled and sliced
1	medium cucumber, sliced
4	cups torn romaine
4	cups torn leaf lettuce
1	small red onion, sliced and separated into rings
1/4	cup orange juice
2	tablespoons balsamic vinegar
1-1/2	teaspoons sugar
1/4	teaspoon salt
1/8	teaspoon pepper
3	tablespoons canola oil
1	cup seasoned salad croutons

Place orange and cucumber slices around the bottom sides of a straight-sided glass salad bowl. Cut any of the remaining orange and cucumber slices in half. Place in another bowl. Add the lettuce and onion.

In a jar with a tight-fitting lid, combine the orange juice, vinegar, sugar, salt, pepper and oil; shake well. Pour over lettuce mixture and toss gently to coat; carefully spoon into salad bowl. Sprinkle with croutons. **YIELD: 8 SERVINGS.**

NUTRITION FACTS: 1 cup equals 111 calories, 6 g fat (1 g saturated fat), trace cholesterol, 141 mg sodium, 13 g carbohydrate, 3 g fiber, 2 g protein. **DIABETIC EXCHANGES:** 1 vegetable, 1 fat, 1/2 fruit.

frozen cherry salad ⒻⓁⓈⓂ

Pretty slices of this refreshing salad are dotted with colorful cherries for a festive look. It can be prepared ahead and frozen, so it's perfect for entertaining during the holidays.
—*Gail Sykora, Menomonee Falls, Wisconsin*

1	package (8 ounces) cream cheese, softened
1	carton (8 ounces) frozen whipped topping, thawed
1	can (21 ounces) cherry pie filling
2	cans (11 ounces *each*) mandarin oranges, drained

Maraschino cherries and orange wedges, optional

In a large bowl, combine the cream cheese and whipped topping. Stir in pie filling. Set aside 1/4 cup oranges for garnish. Fold remaining oranges into cream cheese mixture.

Transfer to a 9-in. x 5-in. loaf pan. Cover and freeze overnight. Remove from freezer 15 minutes before cutting. Garnish with the reserved mandarin oranges, cherries and oranges if desired. **YIELD: 12 SERVINGS.**

NUTRITION FACTS: 1 serving (prepared with fat-free cream cheese, reduced-fat whipped topping and reduced-sugar pie filling and without maraschino cherries and oranges) equals 137 calories, 3 g fat (0 saturated fat), 2 mg cholesterol, 111 mg sodium, 24 g carbohydrate, 0 fiber, 3 g protein. **DIABETIC EXCHANGES:** 1 starch, 1/2 fruit, 1/2 fat.

frozen cherry salad

cottage cheese cantaloupe salad Ⓜ

You can easily wedge this pretty melon salad into any meal plan. The recipe for this refreshing and healthful treat is perfect for a light luncheon. For variety, drizzle a little reduced-fat French salad dressing over the sweet combination of cantaloupe, cottage cheese, granola, raisins and nuts.

—*Margaret Allen, Abingdon, Virginia*

    2 cups (16 ounces) 1% cottage cheese
  1/2 cup raisins
  1/4 cup chopped walnuts
    1 medium cantaloupe, quartered and seeded
  1/4 cup reduced-fat granola
    2 kiwifruit, peeled and sliced
Leaf lettuce

In a small bowl, combine the cottage cheese, raisins and walnuts. Spoon into the cantaloupe wedges. Sprinkle with granola; top with kiwi. Serve immediately on lettuce-lined plates. **YIELD: 4 SERVINGS.**

NUTRITION FACTS: 1 cantaloupe salad equals 282 calories, 7 g fat (1 g saturated fat), 5 mg cholesterol, 500 mg sodium, 41 g carbohydrate, 4 g fiber, 18 g protein. **DIABETIC EXCHANGES:** 2-1/2 fruit, 2 very lean meat, 1 fat, 1/2 starch.

cottage cheese cantaloupe salad

black-eyed pea salad

black-eyed pea salad Ⓜ

To create a new and interesting side dish, I added small pasta shells to my famous black-eyed pea salad. The result is different and delicious. Cucumber and green pepper give this picnic staple a satisfying crunch.

—*Melinda Ewbank, Fairfield, Ohio*

    6 ounces small shell pasta, cooked and drained
    1 can (15 ounces) black-eyed peas, rinsed and drained
    1 cup sliced green onions
  3/4 cup diced seeded peeled cucumber
  3/4 cup diced green pepper
  3/4 cup diced seeded tomato
    1 small jalapeno pepper, seeded and finely chopped
DRESSING:
    3 tablespoons canola oil
  1/4 cup red wine vinegar
    1 teaspoon sugar
    1 teaspoon dried basil
    1 teaspoon chili powder
    1 teaspoon hot pepper sauce
  1/2 teaspoon seasoned salt

In a large salad bowl, combine the first seven ingredients. In a jar with a tight-fitting lid, combine the oil, vinegar, sugar, basil, chili powder, hot pepper sauce and seasoned salt; shake well. Drizzle over salad; toss to coat. Cover and refrigerate for at least 2 hours before serving. **YIELD: 6 SERVINGS.**

NUTRITION FACTS: 1 cup equals 186 calories, 6 g fat (1 g saturated fat), 0 cholesterol, 269 mg sodium, 28 g carbohydrate, 4 g fiber, 6 g protein. **DIABETIC EXCHANGES:** 1-1/2 starch, 1 vegetable, 1 fat.

Editor's Note: *When cutting hot peppers, disposable gloves are recommended. Avoid touching your face.*

vegetable medley (LF) (LC) (ML)

With red pepper slices and green broccoli florets, this colorful combo brightens any table. I use mild seasonings to let the variety of veggie flavors shine through.

—Sara Lindler, Irmo, South Carolina

1	teaspoon chicken bouillon granules
1/4	cup water
1	teaspoon salt
1/4	teaspoon garlic powder
1/4	teaspoon pepper
1	teaspoon plus 1 tablespoon olive oil, *divided*
2	cups fresh broccoli florets
2	medium carrots, thinly sliced
1	large onion, sliced and quartered
1	cup sliced celery
2	medium zucchini, halved lengthwise and thinly sliced
1	medium sweet red pepper, thinly sliced
1	cup sliced fresh mushrooms
2	cups thinly sliced cabbage

In a small saucepan, heat the bouillon and water for 1 minute; stir well. Stir in salt, garlic powder, pepper and 1 teaspoon oil.

In a large nonstick skillet or wok, stir-fry the broccoli, carrots, onion and celery in remaining oil for 2-3 minutes. Add the bouillon mixture; cook and stir for 3 minutes. Add zucchini and red pepper; stir-fry for 3 minutes. Add mushrooms and cabbage; stir-fry 1-2 minutes longer or until crisp-tender. **YIELD: 8 SERVINGS.**

NUTRITION FACTS: 1 cup equals 67 calories, 3 g fat (trace saturated fat), trace cholesterol, 473 mg sodium, 10 g carbohydrate, 3 g fiber, 3 g protein. **DIABETIC EXCHANGES:** 2 vegetable, 1/2 fat.

greek green beans

greek green beans (LC) (ML)

In an effort to eat healthier, I'm trying to serve more vegetables. So I substituted green beans for the pasta in one of my best Greek dishes. It's even better than the original.

—Kathleen Law, Pullman, Washington

1-1/2	pounds fresh green beans, cut into 1-1/2-inch pieces
1	tablespoon olive oil
1	tablespoon minced fresh garlic
1/4	teaspoon salt
1/2	cup crumbled feta cheese

In a microwave-safe dish, combine the beans, oil, garlic and salt. Cover and microwave on high for 5-7 minutes or until tender, stirring twice. Stir in cheese. Serve immediately. **YIELD: 5 SERVINGS.**

NUTRITION FACTS: 3/4 cup equals 107 calories, 6 g fat (3 g saturated fat), 13 mg cholesterol, 285 mg sodium, 9 g carbohydrate, 5 g fiber, 4 g protein. **DIABETIC EXCHANGES:** 2 vegetable, 1 fat.

Editor's Note: This recipe was tested in a 1,100-watt microwave.

vegetable medley

Light COOKING TIP

Purchase fresh green beans with slender green pods that are free of bruises or brown spots. Store unwashed fresh green beans in a resealable plastic bag for up to four days. Wash them just before using, removing strings and ends if necessary.

tortellini caesar salad

tortellini caesar salad ⓜ

The creamy dressing in this salad has plenty of garlic flavor and coats the pasta, romaine and croutons nicely.
—*Tammy Steenbock, Sembach Air Base, Germany*

- 1 package (19 ounces) frozen cheese tortellini
- 1/2 cup mayonnaise
- 1/4 cup milk
- 1/4 cup plus 1/3 cup shredded Parmesan cheese, *divided*
- 2 tablespoons lemon juice
- 2 garlic cloves, minced
- 8 cups torn romaine
- 1 cup seasoned salad croutons

Halved cherry tomatoes, optional

Cook tortellini according to package directions. Meanwhile, in a small bowl, combine the mayonnaise, milk, 1/4 cup Parmesan cheese, lemon juice and garlic.

Drain tortellini and rinse in cold water; transfer to a large bowl. Add romaine and remaining Parmesan. Just before serving, drizzle with dressing; toss to coat. Top with the croutons and tomatoes if desired. **YIELD: 10 SERVINGS.**

NUTRITION FACTS: 1 serving (prepared with fat-free mayonnaise and fat-free milk and without tomatoes) equals 144 calories, 4 g fat (0 saturated fat), 14 mg cholesterol, 318 mg sodium, 18 g carbohydrate, 1 g fiber, 8 g protein. **DIABETIC EXCHANGES:** 1 starch, 1 vegetable, 1 fat.

zippy vegetable soup ⒧ⓕ ⓜ

A blend of tender vegetables adds garden-fresh goodness to this robust soup. Use a spicier salsa to give it a little extra zip.
—*Michelle Nichol, Bedford, Nova Scotia*

- 1/2 cup *each* chopped onion and chopped green pepper
- 1/2 cup thinly sliced carrot
- 1 teaspoon canola oil
- 1 can (16 ounces) kidney beans, rinsed and drained
- 1 can (14-1/2 ounces) diced tomatoes, undrained
- 1 cup water
- 1/4 cup salsa
- 4 teaspoons fat-free sour cream

In a large saucepan, saute the onion, green pepper and carrot in oil until tender. Add the beans, tomatoes, water and salsa.

Bring to a boil; reduce the heat. Cover and simmer for 20-25 minutes or until vegetables are tender. Top each serving with a teaspoon of sour cream. **YIELD: 4 SERVINGS.**

NUTRITION FACTS: 1 cup equals 195 calories, 2 g fat (0 saturated fat), trace cholesterol, 290 mg sodium, 35 g carbohydrate, 0 fiber, 10 g protein. **DIABETIC EXCHANGES:** 2 starch, 1 vegetable, 1/2 fat.

barbecued baked beans

To dress up convenient canned pork and beans, our home economists start with bottled barbecue sauce, then stir in brown sugar, vinegar, Liquid Smoke and spices. These hearty oven-baked beans will become a most-requested dish at your next summer picnic or potluck.
—*Taste of Home Test Kitchen*

- 1/2 cup finely chopped onion
- 2 garlic cloves, minced
- 2 teaspoons canola oil
- 4 cans (15 ounces *each*) pork and beans
- 3/4 cup barbecue sauce
- 1/4 cup packed brown sugar
- 2 tablespoons *each* lemon juice and balsamic vinegar
- 2 tablespoons chili powder
- 2 tablespoons finely chopped jalapeno pepper
- 1/2 to 1 teaspoon cayenne pepper
- 1/8 teaspoon Liquid Smoke, optional

In a Dutch oven, saute onion and garlic in oil until tender. Stir in the next eight ingredients. Add the Liquid Smoke if desired.

Bake, uncovered, at 325° for 1-1/2 to 2 hours or until thickened and bubbly. **YIELD: 11 SERVINGS.**

NUTRITION FACTS: 1/2 cup equals 205 calories, 4 g fat (1 g saturated fat), 6 mg cholesterol, 656 mg sodium, 38 g carbohydrate, 8 g fiber, 7 g protein. **DIABETIC EXCHANGES:** 2-1/2 starch, 1/2 fat.

Editor's Note: When cutting hot peppers, disposable gloves are recommended. Avoid touching your face.

hominy bean salad

hominy bean salad Ⓜ

Chock-full of beans and fresh vegetables, this colorful salad is perfect for pleasing a crowd. Save any leftover beans or veggies to throw into a simmering pot of chili or soup.
—De Loris Lawson, Carthage, Missouri

2 cups fresh green beans, cut into 2-inch pieces
1 can (16 ounces) kidney beans, rinsed and drained
1 can (15-1/2 ounces) hominy, rinsed and drained
1 can (15 ounces) black beans, rinsed and drained
1 cup thinly sliced celery
1 cup thinly sliced red onion
1 medium sweet red pepper, julienned
1/2 cup white wine vinegar
1/2 cup minced fresh cilantro
1/4 cup olive oil
2 teaspoons sugar
1 garlic clove, minced
1/2 teaspoon salt
1/2 teaspoon coarsely ground pepper

Place green beans in a saucepan and cover with water. Bring to a boil. Cook, uncovered, for 8-10 minutes or until crisp-tender; drain and rinse in cold water.

In a serving bowl, combine the green beans, kidney beans, hominy, black beans, celery, onion and red pepper.

In a jar with a tight-fitting lid, combine remaining ingredients; shake well. Pour over vegetables and stir gently to coat. Cover and refrigerate for at least 1 hour. YIELD: 12 SERVINGS.

NUTRITION FACTS: 3/4 cup equals 146 calories, 5 g fat (1 g saturated fat), 0 cholesterol, 425 mg sodium, 20 g carbohydrate, 6 g fiber, 5 g protein. DIABETIC EXCHANGES: 1 starch, 1 vegetable, 1 fat.

pasta bean soup Ⓜ

My family loves this soup during our cold New England winters. It's very thick and filling.
—Beverly Ballaro, Lynnfield, Massachusetts

1 large onion, chopped
1 large carrot, chopped
1 celery rib, chopped
2 tablespoons olive oil
3 garlic cloves, minced
4 cups vegetable *or* chicken broth
3/4 cup uncooked small pasta shells
2 teaspoons sugar
1-1/2 teaspoons Italian seasoning
1/4 teaspoon crushed red pepper flakes
2 cans (15 ounces *each*) white kidney *or* cannellini beans, rinsed and drained
1 can (28 ounces) crushed tomatoes
3 tablespoons grated Parmesan cheese

In a Dutch oven, saute the onion, carrot and celery in oil until crisp-tender. Add garlic; saute 1 minute longer. Add the broth, pasta shells, sugar, Italian seasoning and red pepper flakes.

Bring to a boil. Reduce the heat; simmer, uncovered, for 15 minutes or until pasta is tender. Add the beans and tomatoes; simmer, uncovered, for 5 minutes. Garnish with Parmesan cheese. YIELD: 6 SERVINGS.

NUTRITION FACTS: 1-1/3 cups equals 295 calories, 7 g fat (1 g saturated fat), 2 mg cholesterol, 1,208 mg sodium, 48 g carbohydrate, 9 g fiber, 13 g protein. DIABETIC EXCHANGES: 3 vegetable, 2 starch, 1 very lean meat, 1 fat.

pasta bean soup

bacon-corn stuffed peppers ⓁⒻ

Filled with corn, salsa, green onions, mozzarella cheese and bacon, these grilled pepper halves are sure to liven up your next cookout. They have a wonderful taste and give a fun twist to the usual corn on the cob.

—Mitzi Sentiff, Alexandria, Virginia

2	cups frozen corn, thawed
1/3	cup salsa
6	green onions, chopped
1	medium green pepper, halved and seeded
1	medium sweet red pepper, halved and seeded
1/4	cup shredded part-skim mozzarella cheese
2	bacon strips, cooked and crumbled

Additional salsa, optional

In a large bowl, combine the corn, salsa and onions. Spoon into pepper halves. Place each stuffed pepper half on a piece of heavy-duty foil (about 18 in. x 12 in.). Fold foil around peppers and seal tightly.

Grill, covered, over medium heat for 25-30 minutes or until peppers are crisp-tender. Carefully open packets. Sprinkle with cheese and bacon. Return to the grill for 3-5 minutes or until cheese is melted. Serve with additional salsa if desired. YIELD: 4 SERVINGS.

NUTRITION FACTS: 1 stuffed pepper (prepared with part-skim mozzarella cheese and without additional salsa) equals 120 calories, 2 g fat (1 g saturated fat), 3 mg cholesterol, 151 mg sodium, 23 g carbohydrate, 4 g fiber, 4 g protein. DIABETIC EXCHANGES: 1 starch, 1 vegetable, 1/2 fat.

bacon-corn stuffed peppers

garlic twice-baked potatoes

garlic twice-baked potatoes ⓂⓁ

You'll only have to announce dinner once when these twice-baked potatoes are on the menu! Their aroma is sure to make everyone eager to come to the table. Garlic and rosemary add herbal goodness to the mashed potato filling. A sprinkling of paprika serves as a colorful garnish.

—Taste of Home Test Kitchen

6	medium baking potatoes
1	whole garlic bulb
1	teaspoon olive oil
2	tablespoons butter, softened
1/2	cup fat-free milk
1/2	cup buttermilk
1-1/2	teaspoons minced fresh rosemary *or* 1/2 teaspoon dried rosemary, crushed
1/2	teaspoon salt
1/8	teaspoon pepper

Paprika

Bake the potatoes at 400° for 45-55 minutes or until tender. Meanwhile remove papery outer skin from garlic (do not peel or separate cloves). Place garlic in a double thickness of heavy-duty foil. Drizzle with oil. Wrap foil around garlic.

Bake at 400° for 30-35 minutes or until softened. Cool for 10 minutes. Cut top off garlic head, leaving root end intact. Squeeze softened garlic into a small bowl; set aside.

Cut a thin slice off the top of each potato and discard. Scoop out the pulp, leaving a thin shell. In a large bowl, mash the pulp with butter. Stir in the milk, buttermilk, rosemary, salt, pepper and roasted garlic.

Pipe or spoon into potato shells. Place on an ungreased baking sheet. Bake at 425° for 20-25 minutes or until heated through. Sprinkle with paprika. YIELD: 6 SERVINGS.

NUTRITION FACTS: 1 stuffed potato equals 194 calories, 5 g fat (3 g saturated fat), 11 mg cholesterol, 277 mg sodium, 34 g carbohydrate, 3 g fiber, 5 g protein. DIABETIC EXCHANGES: 2 starch, 1 fat.

celery zucchini soup (ML)

There's a harvest of fresh flavor in this pleasant celery soup. I concocted the recipe at the end of the growing season with leftover vegetables from my garden.
—Alyson Sprague, Sewickley, Pennsylvania

3	green onions, thinly sliced
2	garlic cloves, minced
2	tablespoons butter
4	celery ribs, chopped
2	medium carrots, chopped
2	cups water
1	tablespoon reduced-sodium chicken bouillon granules *or* 1-1/2 vegetable bouillon cubes
3/4	teaspoon salt
3/4	teaspoon dried thyme
5	medium red potatoes, cut into small chunks (about 1 pound)
3	cups fat-free milk
2	cups shredded zucchini
2	tablespoons cornstarch
1/4	cup cold water

In a large saucepan, saute onions and garlic in butter until tender. Add celery and carrots; cook and stir for 4 minutes. Stir in the water, bouillon, salt and thyme. Add potatoes. Bring to a boil.

Reduce heat; cover and simmer about 15 minutes or until potatoes are tender. Stir in milk and zucchini. Bring to a boil. In a small bowl, combine cornstarch and cold water until smooth. Gradually whisk into soup. Return to a boil; cook and stir for 2 minutes or until slightly thickened. YIELD: 6 SERVINGS.

NUTRITION FACTS: 1-1/2 cups equals 175 calories, 4 g fat (2 g saturated fat), 13 mg cholesterol, 651 mg sodium, 28 g carbohydrate, 3 g fiber, 7 g protein. DIABETIC EXCHANGES: 1 starch, 1 vegetable, 1 fat, 1/2 fat-free milk.

tangy vegetable pasta salad (LF) (ML)

The variety of ingredients in my pasta salad will take your taste buds in all different directions. It's surprising how well the zippy citrus and raw vegetable flavors blend together.
—Wilma Jones, Mobile, Alabama

2-1/4	cups uncooked spiral pasta
2	tablespoons lemon juice
3	plum tomatoes, sliced
1/2	cup chopped green pepper
1/2	cup sliced radishes
1/2	cup chopped peeled cucumber

DRESSING:

1/3	cup picante V8 juice
1/4	cup orange juice
2	tablespoons lemon juice
2	tablespoons chopped green onion
1	tablespoon canola oil
1-1/2	teaspoons sugar
1	teaspoon grated lemon peel
1	teaspoon grated orange peel
1/2	teaspoon salt
1/2	teaspoon dill weed

Cook pasta according to package directions, adding the lemon juice to the water. Drain and cool.

In a large bowl, combine the pasta, tomatoes, green pepper, radishes and cucumber. In a jar with a tight-fitting lid, combine the dressing ingredients; cover and shake well. Pour over salad; toss to coat. Cover and refrigerate until serving. YIELD: 6 SERVINGS.

NUTRITION FACTS: 1 cup equals 184 calories, 3 g fat (trace saturated fat), 0 cholesterol, 254 mg sodium, 31 g carbohydrate, 2 g fiber, 8 g protein. DIABETIC EXCHANGES: 1-1/2 starch, 1 vegetable, 1/2 fat.

tangy vegetable pasta salad

confetti bean salad

confetti bean salad ⓂⓁ

This medley of beans won the enthusiastic approval of my husband. The peas and corn add crunch and color.

—Bonnie McKinsey, Greenville, South Carolina

1	can (16 ounces) kidney beans, rinsed and drained
1	can (15 ounces) garbanzo beans *or* chickpeas, rinsed and drained
1	can (14-1/2 ounces) Italian diced tomatoes, drained
1-1/2	cups *each* frozen peas and frozen corn
1/2	cup chopped onion
1/2	cup chopped green pepper
3	tablespoons red wine vinegar
2	tablespoons olive oil
1	garlic clove, minced
1/2	teaspoon salt
1/4	teaspoon pepper

In a large bowl, combine the first seven ingredients. In a small bowl, combine the vinegar, oil, garlic, salt and pepper until blended. Pour over bean mixture; toss gently to coat. Cover and refrigerate for at least 4 hours. **YIELD: 10 SERVINGS.**

NUTRITION FACTS: 3/4 cup equals 176 calories, 4 g fat (trace saturated fat), 0 cholesterol, 358 mg sodium, 30 g carbohydrate, 8 g fiber, 7 g protein. **DIABETIC EXCHANGES:** 1-1/2 starch, 1 vegetable, 1 fat.

light scalloped potatoes ⓁⒻ ⓂⓁ

Even when made with lighter ingredients, this cheesy potato dish is pure comfort food.

—Tamie Foley, Thousand Oaks, California

6	medium potatoes, peeled and thinly sliced
3	cups water
4	reduced-sodium chicken bouillon cubes
1	garlic clove, minced
1/2	cup grated Parmesan cheese
Minced fresh parsley, optional	

Place potatoes in a greased 2-qt. baking dish that has been coated with cooking spray. In a small saucepan, heat the water, bouillon and garlic until bouillon is dissolved; pour over potatoes. Sprinkle with Parmesan cheese.

Bake, uncovered, at 350° for 1-1/4 to 1-1/2 hours or until tender. Let stand 10 minutes before serving. Sprinkle with fresh parsley if desired. Serve with a slotted spoon. **YIELD: 6 SERVINGS.**

NUTRITION FACTS: 1/2-cup serving equals 175 calories, 3 g fat (0 saturated fat), 7 mg cholesterol, 168 mg sodium, 32 g carbohydrate, 0 fiber, 3 g protein. **DIABETIC EXCHANGES:** 2 starch, 1/2 fat.

tangy green beans ⓁⒻ ⓁⒸ ⓂⓁ

This vegetable side dish is delicately dressed with white wine vinegar and subtle mustard and garlic seasonings, rather than swimming in butter and salt.

—Taste of Home Test Kitchen

1-1/2	pounds fresh green beans, trimmed
1/3	cup diced sweet red pepper
4-1/2	teaspoons olive oil
4-1/2	teaspoons water
1-1/2	teaspoons white wine vinegar
1-1/2	teaspoons spicy brown mustard
3/4	teaspoon salt
1/4	teaspoon pepper
1/8	teaspoon garlic powder

Place beans and red pepper in a basket over 1 in. of boiling water in a saucepan. Cover and steam for 7-8 minutes or until crisp-tender.

Meanwhile, in a small bowl, whisk together the remaining ingredients. Transfer bean mixture to a serving bowl; add vinaigrette and stir to coat. **YIELD: 9 SERVINGS.**

NUTRITION FACTS: 1/2 cup equals 43 calories, 2 g fat (trace saturated fat), 0 cholesterol, 207 mg sodium, 5 g carbohydrate, 3 g fiber, 1 g protein. **DIABETIC EXCHANGES:** 1 vegetable, 1/2 fat.

tangy green beans

easy gazpacho

easy gazpacho ⓜ

There's plenty of garden goodness in every bowl of this fresh-tasting soup. Served chilled, it's the perfect accompaniment to a summer meal.
—*Marlene Muckenhirn, Delano, Minnesota*

2-1/2 cups reduced-sodium tomato juice
   3 tablespoons white vinegar
   3 tablespoons olive oil
   2 garlic cloves, minced
1/4 teaspoon salt
   2 to 3 drops hot pepper sauce
   4 large tomatoes, chopped and *divided*
   1 medium onion, chopped
   1 medium cucumber, peeled, seeded and chopped
   1 medium green pepper, chopped
1/4 cup fat-free croutons

In a blender, combine the tomato juice, vinegar, oil, garlic, salt, hot pepper sauce and half of the tomatoes; cover and process until smooth. Transfer to a bowl.

Add the onion, cucumber, green pepper and remaining tomatoes. Cover and refrigerate for 4 hours or until chilled. Garnish with croutons. YIELD: 4 SERVINGS.

NUTRITION FACTS: 1-1/2 cups equals 203 calories, 11 g fat (2 g saturated fat), trace cholesterol, 285 mg sodium, 24 g carbohydrate, 4 g fiber, 4 g protein. DIABETIC EXCHANGES: 5 vegetable, 2 fat.

roasted rosemary cauliflower ⒧ⓛⓒⓜ

Roasting the cauliflower really brings out its essence in this side dish. Even folks who aren't cauliflower lovers like it this way.
—*Joann Fritzler, Belen, New Mexico*

   1 head medium head cauliflower, about 2-1/2 pounds, cut into 1-inch florets
4-1/2 teaspoons olive oil

   2 teaspoons minced fresh rosemary *or*
3/4 teaspoon dried rosemary, crushed
1/2 teaspoon salt

In a large bowl, toss cauliflower with the oil, rosemary and salt until well coated. Arrange in a single layer in an ungreased 15-in. x 10-in. x 1-in. baking pan.

Bake, uncovered, at 450° for 25-30 minutes or until cauliflower is lightly browned and tender, stirring occasionally. YIELD: 8 SERVINGS.

NUTRITION FACTS: 3/4 cup equals 44 calories, 3 g fat (trace saturated fat), 0 cholesterol, 161 mg sodium, 4 g carbohydrate, 3 g fiber, 2 g protein. DIABETIC EXCHANGES: 1 vegetable, 1/2 fat.

mock caesar salad ⓛⓒ ⓜ

This lightened-up version of the classic is a tasty complement to a soup or main dish. Best of all, the thick, creamy dressing has all the flavor you'd expect with just a fraction of the fat.
—*Sue Yaeger, Boone, Iowa*

1/3 cup fat-free plain yogurt
1/4 cup reduced-fat mayonnaise
   1 tablespoon red wine vinegar
   2 teaspoons Dijon mustard
   1 teaspoon Worcestershire sauce
1/4 teaspoon garlic powder
1/8 teaspoon pepper
   6 cups torn romaine
1/2 cup fat-free salad croutons
   2 tablespoons shredded Parmesan cheese

In a small bowl, whisk together the first seven ingredients. In a salad bowl, combine the romaine, croutons and cheese. Drizzle with dressing; toss to coat. YIELD: 5 SERVINGS.

NUTRITION FACTS: 1-1/4 cups equals 90 calories, 5 g fat (1 g saturated fat), 7 mg cholesterol, 299 mg sodium, 9 g carbohydrate, 1 g fiber, 4 g protein. DIABETIC EXCHANGES: 1 fat, 1/2 starch.

mock caesar salad

melon turkey salad

With its combination of tender chunks of turkey, sweet melon balls and juicy grapes, this salad is a winner at our ladies' club.
—Carolyn Zimmerman, Fairbury, Illinois

4	medium cantaloupes, halved and seeded
4	cups cubed cooked turkey breast
1-1/2	cups seedless red grapes, halved
1	cup chopped celery
1/2	cup fat-free plain yogurt
1/4	cup reduced-fat mayonnaise
1	teaspoon lemon juice
1/2	teaspoon ground ginger
1/8	teaspoon salt
1/2	cup chopped unsalted dry roasted cashews

Make melon balls from one cantaloupe half; refrigerate the remaining cantaloupe halves. In a large bowl, combine the turkey, grapes, celery and cantaloupe balls.

In a small bowl, combine the yogurt, mayonnaise, lemon juice, ginger and salt. Pour over turkey mixture and stir gently to coat. Cover and refrigerate for 1 hour.

Stir in cashews just before serving. Spoon 1 cup salad into each cantaloupe half. **YIELD: 7 SERVINGS.**

NUTRITION FACTS: 1 cup equals 157 calories, 5 g fat (2 g saturated fat), 3 mg cholesterol, 243 mg sodium, 21 g carbohydrate, 3 g fiber, 7 g protein. **DIABETIC EXCHANGES:** 3 very lean meat, 2-1/2 fruit, 1-1/2 fat.

melon turkey salad

roasted corn on the cob

roasted corn on the cob

I've been grilling corn on the cob this way for years. The foil makes cleanup a breeze.
—Sandy Szwarc, Albuquerque, New Mexico

8	medium ears sweet corn, husks removed
	Refrigerated butter-flavored spray
2	tablespoons butter, melted
2	tablespoons prepared horseradish
2	tablespoons Dijon mustard
2	garlic cloves, minced
1/2	teaspoon salt
1/8	teaspoon pepper
1/8	teaspoon paprika

Spray eight 12-in. x 10-in. pieces of foil with cooking spray. Place one ear of corn on each piece of foil; spritz corn evenly with butter-flavored spray. Fold foil over corn and seal tightly.

Grill, covered, over medium indirect heat or bake at 400° for 25-30 minutes or until corn is tender. Combine the butter, horseradish, mustard, garlic, salt and pepper; brush over corn. Sprinkle with paprika. **YIELD: 8 SERVINGS.**

NUTRITION FACTS: 1 seasoned ear of corn equals 115 calories, 4 g fat (2 g saturated fat), 8 mg cholesterol, 291 mg sodium, 20 g carbohydrate, 2 g fiber, 3 g protein. **DIABETIC EXCHANGES:** 1-1/2 starch, 1/2 fat.

Light
COOKING TIP

Corn on the cob is a classic summertime side dish. But add too much butter or salt and this healthful vegetable becomes a nutritional no-no. Instead, experiment with a variety of herbs or seasonings. Basil and rosemary are a delicious combination.

grilled corn pasta salad (ML)

A perfect warm-weather salad, this colorful dish is especially tasty when sweet corn, tomatoes and zucchini are in season. The garden-fresh ingredients are lightly dressed in mild basil vinegar and oil, plus a blend of other herbs and seasonings.
—Taste of Home Test Kitchen

4	large ears sweet corn in husks
1-1/2	cups uncooked penne pasta
2	cups cherry tomatoes
1	medium zucchini, thinly sliced
1	can (2-1/4 ounces) sliced ripe olives, drained
1/3	cup white wine vinegar
2	tablespoons olive oil
1	tablespoon minced fresh basil *or*
	1 teaspoon dried basil
1	teaspoon *each* sugar and salt
1	teaspoon salt
1/2	teaspoon ground mustard
1/4	teaspoon each garlic powder and pepper

Carefully peel back corn husks to within 1 in. of bottom; remove silk. Rewrap corn in husks and secure with kitchen string. Place in a large kettle; cover with cold water. Soak for 20 minutes; drain. Grill corn, covered, over medium heat for 25-30 minutes or until tender, turning often.

Meanwhile, cook pasta according to package directions; drain and rinse in cold water. When corn is cool enough to handle, remove kernels from cobs and place in a large bowl. Add the pasta, tomatoes, zucchini and olives.

lentil vegetable soup

In a jar with a tight-fitting lid, combine remaining ingredients; shake well. Pour over salad and toss gently to coat. Cover and refrigerate until serving. **YIELD: 8 SERVINGS.**

NUTRITION FACTS: 1 cup equals 164 calories, 6 g fat (1 g saturated fat), 0 cholesterol, 382 mg sodium, 27 g carbohydrate, 3 g fiber, 5 g protein. **DIABETIC EXCHANGES:** 1-1/2 starch, 1 fat.

lentil vegetable soup (ML)

Here is one good-for-you dish that our kids really enjoy. Serve this tasty soup as a hearty meatless dinner entree or pair it with a favorite sandwich for lunch.
—Joy Maynard, St. Ignatius, Montana

3	cans (14-1/2 ounces *each*) vegetable broth
1	medium onion, chopped
1/2	cup dried lentils, rinsed
1/2	cup uncooked long grain brown rice
1/2	cup tomato juice
1	can (5-1/2 ounces) spicy hot V8 juice
1	tablespoon reduced-sodium soy sauce
1	tablespoon canola oil
1	medium potato, peeled and cubed
1	medium tomato, cubed
1	medium carrot, sliced
1	celery rib, sliced

In a large saucepan, combine first eight ingredients. Bring to a boil. Reduce heat; cover and simmer for 30 minutes.

Add the potato, tomato, carrot and celery; cover and simmer 30 minutes longer or until rice and vegetables are tender. **YIELD: 6 SERVINGS.**

NUTRITION FACTS: 1 cup equals 195 calories, 4 g fat (0 saturated fat), 0 cholesterol, 1,144 mg sodium, 34 g carbohydrate, 6 g fiber, 9 g protein. **DIABETIC EXCHANGES:** 2 starch, 1 vegetable, 1/2 fat.

grilled corn pasta salad

tempting tomato cups (LF) (ML)

For as long as I can remember, I've eaten this pretty salad in the summer when fresh tomatoes are so good. Brimming with a delicious filling, it makes a wonderful light lunch or can replace a green salad at dinner.
—Carla Browning, Fort Walton Beach, Florida

3	large tomatoes
1/2	cup crushed saltines (about 15 crackers)
1/3	cup chopped celery
1/3	cup chopped green pepper
1/4	cup chopped onion
1/4	cup mayonnaise
1/2	teaspoon garlic salt, optional
1/8	teaspoon pepper

Sliced ripe olives, optional

Cut a thin slice from the top of each tomato. Leaving a 1/4-in.-thick shell, scoop out pulp (discard pulp or save for another use). Invert tomatoes onto paper towels to drain.

In a large bowl, combine the cracker crumbs, celery, green pepper, onion, mayonnaise, garlic salt if desired and pepper; mix well. Spoon into tomatoes. Refrigerate until serving. Garnish with olives if desired. **YIELD: 3 SERVINGS.**

NUTRITION FACTS: 1 tomato cup (prepared with low-sodium saltines and fat-free mayonnaise and without garlic salt and olives) equals 129 calories, 2 g fat, 0 cholesterol, 284 mg sodium, 25 g carbohydrate, 3 g protein. **DIABETIC EXCHANGES:** 1 starch, 1 vegetable, 1/2 fat.

italian vegetable salad

tempting tomato cups

italian vegetable salad (LC) (ML)

Even our two small children eat their vegetables when I serve this colorful, nutritious combination. To make it a main dish, I'll stir in pepperoni slices and cooled cooked pasta into the crunchy, creamy blend.
—Debbie Laubach, La Prairie, Minnesota

5	cups fresh broccoli florets (1 large bunch)
5	cups fresh cauliflowerets (1 small head)
4	plum tomatoes, chopped
1	medium cucumber, peeled and sliced
1	medium sweet onion, thinly sliced
1	cup sliced fresh carrots
2	cans (2-1/4 ounces *each*) sliced ripe olives, drained
1/2	cup pimiento-stuffed olives
1	bottle (8 ounces) Italian salad dressing
1	bottle (8 ounces) creamy Italian salad dressing
2	cups (8 ounces) shredded part-skim mozzarella cheese

In a large salad bowl, combine the first eight ingredients. Combine salad dressings; pour over vegetable mixture and toss to coat. Cover and refrigerate for at least 4 hours. Stir in cheese just before serving. **YIELD: 14 SERVINGS.**

NUTRITION FACTS: 1 serving (prepared with fat-free salad dressings) equals 121 calories, 6 g fat (0 saturated fat), 10 mg cholesterol, 531 mg sodium, 11 g carbohydrate, 0 fiber, 6 g protein. **DIABETIC EXCHANGES:** 2 vegetable, 1-1/2 fat.

balsamic roasted red potatoes ⓜ

My family loves potatoes, and I fix them many different ways. This tasty version is one of our favorites. Well-seasoned with garlic, thyme, nutmeg and rosemary, plus balsamic vinegar, these potatoes are sure to stand out at any meal.

—Bev Bosveld, Waupun, Wisconsin

2	pounds small red potatoes, quartered
1	tablespoon finely chopped green onion
6	garlic cloves, minced
2	tablespoons olive oil
1	teaspoon dried thyme
1	teaspoon dried rosemary, crushed
1/8	teaspoon ground nutmeg
1/4	cup balsamic vinegar
3/4	teaspoon salt
1/4	teaspoon pepper

In a large nonstick skillet, combine the potatoes, onion and garlic; cook over medium-high heat in oil for 2-3 minutes or until heated through. Stir in the thyme, rosemary and nutmeg. Cook and stir for 2-3 minutes longer or until heated through.

Transfer to a 15-in. x 10-in. x 1-in. baking pan coated with cooking spray. Bake at 400° for 25-30 minutes or until potatoes are golden and almost tender. Add the vinegar, salt and pepper; toss well. Bake 5-8 minutes longer or until potatoes are tender. **YIELD: 6 SERVINGS.**

NUTRITION FACTS: 3/4 cup equals 184 calories, 5 g fat (1 g saturated fat), 0 cholesterol, 306 mg sodium, 33 g carbohydrate, 3 g fiber, 3 g protein. **DIABETIC EXCHANGES:** 2 starch, 1 fat.

kiwi-strawberry spinach salad ⓛⓢ ⓜ

This pretty salad is always a hit when I serve it! The recipe came from a cookbook, but I "doctored" it to add a personal touch. Sometimes just a small change in ingredients can make a big difference.

—Laura Pounds, Andover, Kansas

12	cups torn fresh spinach
2	pints fresh strawberries, halved
4	kiwifruit, peeled and cut into 1/4-inch slices
1/4	cup canola oil
1/4	cup raspberry vinegar
1/4	teaspoon Worcestershire sauce
1/3	cup sugar
1/4	teaspoon paprika
2	green onions, chopped
2	tablespoons sesame seeds, toasted
1	tablespoon poppy seeds

In a large salad bowl, combine the spinach, strawberries and kiwi. In a blender, combine the oil, vinegar, Worcestershire sauce, sugar and paprika; cover and process for 30 seconds or until blended. Add the onions, sesame seeds and poppy seeds. Pour over salad; toss to coat. **YIELD: 12 SERVINGS.**

NUTRITION FACTS: 1 cup equals 121 calories, 6 g fat (trace saturated fat), 0 cholesterol, 64 mg sodium, 16 g carbohydrate, 4 g fiber, 3 g protein. **DIABETIC EXCHANGES:** 1 fruit, 1 fat, 1/2 vegetable.

kiwi-strawberry spinach salad

new waldorf salad

vegetable couscous (ML)

Looking for a new way to serve vegetables? These tiny pasta granules act like a magnet, pulling together the flavors of the chicken broth and vitamin-rich veggies. Carrots, celery, peppers and zucchini add fresh crunch and bright color.
—Taste of Home Test Kitchen

2	medium carrots
1/2	cup diced celery
1	medium onion, finely chopped
1/4	cup julienned sweet yellow pepper
1/4	cup julienned sweet red pepper
2	tablespoons olive oil
1	medium zucchini, diced
1/4	cup minced fresh basil *or* 4 teaspoons dried basil
1/4	teaspoon garlic salt
1/8	teaspoon pepper

Dash hot pepper sauce

1	cup uncooked couscous
1-1/2	cups chicken broth

In a large skillet, saute the carrots, celery, onion and peppers in oil for 5-6 minutes or until vegetables are crisp-tender. Add the next five ingredients.

Stir in couscous. Add broth; bring to a boil. Cover and remove from the heat; let stand for 5-8 minutes. Fluff with a fork and serve immediately. **YIELD: 4 SERVINGS.**

NUTRITION FACTS: 1-1/4 cups equals 272 calories, 8 g fat (1 g saturated fat), 0 cholesterol, 513 mg sodium, 43 g carbohydrate, 4 g fiber, 8 g protein. **DIABETIC EXCHANGES:** 2 starch, 1 lean meat, 1 fat.

new waldorf salad (LS) (ML)

A nice blend of fruits and nuts gives this invigorating salad a delightful texture. The citrusy topping dresses it up perfectly. It's easy to fix and good for you, too.
—Marie Engwall, Willmar, Minnesota

1	medium unpeeled red apple, chopped
1	medium unpeeled green apple, chopped
1	medium unpeeled pear, chopped
1/2	cup green grapes
1/4	cup raisins
1/4	cup slivered almonds, toasted
1	carton (6 ounces) reduced-fat lemon yogurt
2	teaspoons lemon juice
2	teaspoons orange juice
2	teaspoons honey
1	teaspoon grated orange peel

Lettuce leaves, optional

In a large bowl, combine the apples, pear, grapes, raisins and almonds. In a small bowl, combine the yogurt, lemon and orange juices, honey and orange peel; pour over fruit mixture and stir to coat. Serve immediately in lettuce-lined bowls if desired. **YIELD: 4 SERVINGS.**

NUTRITION FACTS: 1 cup equals 193 calories, 5 g fat (1 g saturated fat), 2 mg cholesterol, 33 mg sodium, 35 g carbohydrate, 4 g fiber, 5 g protein. **DIABETIC EXCHANGES:** 2 fruit, 1/2 fat-free milk, 1/2 fat.

vegetable couscous

sticks 'n' stones salad

sticks 'n' stones salad ⓁⒸ Ⓜ

Sticks of celery and carrots tossed with water chestnuts ("stones") are nicely coated in a dill and Dijon mustard dressing in this dish. This salad is a big hit with our children—it's a great way to get them to eat their vegetables. They love to munch on this snack, and the recipe name makes them giggle.

—Nancy Zicker, Port Orange, Florida

- 5 celery ribs, julienned
- 2 large carrots, julienned
- 1 can (8 ounces) sliced water chestnuts, drained
- 2 tablespoons olive oil
- 2 tablespoons cider vinegar
- 1 teaspoon sugar
- 1 teaspoon Dijon mustard
- 1/2 teaspoon salt
- 1/4 teaspoon dill weed

Place celery and carrots in a saucepan; cover with water. Bring to a boil. Cook, uncovered, for 3-4 minutes; drain and rinse with cold water. Drain thoroughly.

Transfer to a large bowl; add the water chestnuts. In a small bowl, whisk the oil, vinegar, sugar, mustard, salt and dill. Pour over vegetables and toss to coat.
YIELD: 4 SERVINGS.

NUTRITION FACTS: 3/4 cup equals 121 calories, 7 g fat (1 g saturated fat), 0 cholesterol, 396 mg sodium, 14 g carbohydrate, 5 g fiber, 1 g protein. **DIABETIC EXCHANGES:** 3 vegetable, 1 fat.

fresh 'n' fruity salad ⓁⓈ Ⓜ

We love all types of melons, so I'm always experimenting with different ways to serve them. A light dressing brings out the refreshing fruit flavors in this cool salad that's so delightful in warm weather.

—Bernice Morris, Marshfield, Missouri

- 1 can (20 ounces) unsweetened pineapple chunks, drained
- 1 can (15 ounces) unsweetened dark sweet cherries, drained
- 1-1/2 cups cubed cantaloupe
- 1-1/2 cups cubed seeded watermelon
- 1-1/2 cups cubed honeydew

DRESSING:
- 3 tablespoons canola oil
- 3 tablespoons orange juice
- 3 tablespoons lemon juice
- 2 tablespoons sugar
- 1/4 teaspoon paprika

In a large bowl, combine all the fruit. In a small bowl, combine dressing ingredients; pour over fruit and toss to coat. Serve immediately with a slotted spoon. **YIELD: 8 SERVINGS.**

NUTRITION FACTS: 1/2-cup serving equals 140 calories, 6 g fat (0 saturated fat), 0 cholesterol, 8 mg sodium, 24 g carbohydrate, 0 fiber, 1 g protein. **DIABETIC EXCHANGES:** 1-1/2 fruit, 1 fat.

Light COOKING TIP

For another healthful version of fruit salad, mix various fruits, such as grapes, orange sections, chopped pineapple or bananas, with fat-free whipped topping and vanilla yogurt. The yogurt provides bone-building calcium and vitamin D.

fresh 'n' fruity salad

cheesy scalloped potatoes (ML)

The recipe for these creamy homemade potatoes makes use of reduced-fat cheese so it's not so loaded with calories.
—Taste of Home Test Kitchen

4 pounds potatoes, peeled and sliced (about 5 large potatoes)
3 tablespoons all-purpose flour
1-1/2 teaspoons salt
1/4 teaspoon pepper
1-1/4 cups shredded reduced-fat cheddar cheese, *divided*
3 ounces reduced-fat Swiss cheese slices, finely chopped (3/4 cup), *divided*
2 medium onions, finely chopped
1-1/2 cups 2% milk
2 tablespoons minced fresh parsley

Place a third of the potatoes in a shallow 3-qt. baking dish coated with cooking spray. In a small bowl, combine the flour, salt and pepper; sprinkle half over potatoes. Sprinkle with 1/4 cup of each cheese and half of the onions. Repeat layers. Top with remaining potatoes. Pour milk over all.

Cover and bake at 350° for 50-60 minutes or until potatoes are nearly tender. Sprinkle with remaining cheeses. Bake, uncovered, 10 minutes longer or until cheese is melted and potatoes are tender. Sprinkle with parsley. **YIELD: 8 SERVINGS.**

NUTRITION FACTS: 3/4 cup equals 327 calories, 7 g fat (4 g saturated fat), 21 mg cholesterol, 604 mg sodium, 55 g carbohydrate, 5 g fiber, 15 g protein. **DIABETIC EXCHANGES:** 2 starch, 1 lean meat, 1/2 fat.

apple cider salad

apple cider salad (ML)

Whenever I prepare this cool, refreshing salad with crunchy nuts and apples, I'm reminded of my mother. She prepared it every year for Thanksgiving since we always had an abundance of fresh-picked apples on hand.
—Jeannette Mack, Rushville, New York

2 envelopes unflavored gelatin
3-3/4 cups apple cider, *divided*
3 tablespoons lemon juice
3 tablespoons sugar
1/2 teaspoon salt
3-1/2 to 4 cups chopped peeled apples
1 cup chopped walnuts

In a small saucepan, sprinkle gelatin over 1/4 cup of cider; let stand for 2 minutes. Add the lemon juice, sugar, salt and remaining cider. Cook and stir over medium heat until sugar and gelatin are dissolved. Cover and refrigerate until slightly thickened, about 2-1/2 hours.

Fold in apples and walnuts. Transfer to a 2-qt. serving bowl. Cover and refrigerate overnight. **YIELD: 12 SERVINGS.**

NUTRITION FACTS: 1/2-cup serving equals 135 calories, 6 g fat (0 saturated fat), 0 cholesterol, 102 mg sodium, 19 g carbohydrate, 0 fiber, 4 g protein. **DIABETIC EXCHANGES:** 1-1/2 fruit, 1 fat.

cheesy scalloped potatoes

Light
COOKING TIP

Toss in some sliced carrots the next time you make scalloped potatoes. They will add a pretty color and lots of nutrition.

baked stuffed zucchini (LC) (ML)

This recipe proves you don't have to fuss to make a special side dish for two. It's so easy to dress up zucchini halves with this scrumptious mushroom stuffing.
—Sarah Rodgers, Pittsburgh, Pennsylvania

1	medium zucchini
6	large fresh mushrooms, finely chopped
1	green onion, finely chopped
1	tablespoon butter
1/2	cup white wine *or* chicken broth
1/8	teaspoon salt
	Dash white pepper
2	teaspoons grated Parmesan cheese

Cut zucchini in half lengthwise. Scoop out pulp, leaving a 1/4-in. shell. Chop pulp; set shells aside.

In a large nonstick skillet, saute zucchini pulp, mushrooms and onion in butter for 3-4 minutes or until tender. Add wine or broth. Reduce heat; simmer, uncovered, for 10-12 minutes or until liquid has evaporated. Stir in the salt and pepper.

Place zucchini shells in a saucepan and cover with water; bring to a boil. Cook for 2 minutes or until crisp-tender; drain.

Fill shells with mushroom mixture. Sprinkle with cheese. Broil 3-4 in. from the heat for 3-4 minutes or until lightly browned. **YIELD: 2 SERVINGS.**

NUTRITION FACTS: 1 stuffed zucchini half equals 133 calories, 7 g fat (4 g saturated fat), 17 mg cholesterol, 254 mg sodium, 7 g carbohydrate, 2 g fiber, 4 g protein. **DIABETIC EXCHANGES:** 2 vegetable, 1 fat, 1/2 starch.

lemon-maple butternut squash (LF) (LS) (ML)

My mother discovered this healthful recipe that's become a family favorite. We enjoy its bright color, smooth texture and flavorful combination of tangy lemon and sweet maple. It's a great dish to enjoy in the fall.
—Barbara Ballast, Grand Rapids, Michigan

1	large butternut squash (2-1/2 pounds), halved lengthwise and seeded
1/4	cup water
1/4	cup maple syrup
1	tablespoon butter, melted
1	tablespoon lemon juice
1/2	teaspoon grated lemon peel

Place squash cut side down in an ungreased 13-in. x 9-in. baking dish. Add water. Cover and bake at 350° for 50-60 minutes or until tender. Scoop out the squash and place in a large bowl, add the syrup, butter, lemon juice and peel; beat until smooth. **YIELD: 4 SERVINGS.**

NUTRITION FACTS: 3/4 cup equals 186 calories, 3 g fat (2 g saturated fat), 8 mg cholesterol, 41 mg sodium, 42 g carbohydrate, 8 g fiber, 2 g protein. **DIABETIC EXCHANGES:** 2-1/2 starch, 1/2 fat.

tortellini soup (ML)

I like to top bowls of this tasty soup with a little grated Parmesan cheese...and serve it with crusty bread to round out the heartwarming meal.
—Donna Morgan, Hend, Tennessee

2	garlic cloves, minced
1	tablespoon butter
3	cans (14-1/2 ounces *each*) reduced-sodium chicken broth *or* vegetable broth
1	package (9 ounces) refrigerated cheese tortellini
1	can (14-1/2 ounces) diced tomatoes with green chilies, undrained
1	package (10 ounces) frozen chopped spinach, thawed

In a large saucepan, saute garlic in butter until tender. Stir in the broth. Bring to a boil. Add the tortellini; cook for 7-9 minutes or until tender. Stir in the tomatoes and spinach; heat through. **YIELD: 5 SERVINGS.**

NUTRITION FACTS: 1-1/2 cups equals 242 calories, 6 g fat (4 g saturated fat), 25 mg cholesterol, 1,181 mg sodium, 33 g carbohydrate, 4 g fiber, 13 g protein. **DIABETIC EXCHANGES:** 2 vegetable, 1-1/2 starch, 1 lean meat, 1/2 fat.

tortellini soup

corn pasta salad

corn pasta salad

After tasting this chilled salad at a family reunion, I immediately asked the hostess for the recipe. I use tricolor pasta, crunchy corn, red onion and green pepper to give the zippy potluck pleaser plenty of color.
—Bernice Morris, Marshfield, Missouri

2	cups cooked tricolor spiral pasta
1	package (16 ounces) frozen corn, thawed
1	cup chopped celery
1	medium green pepper, chopped
1	cup chopped seeded tomatoes
1/2	cup *each* diced pimientos and chopped red onion
1	cup picante sauce
2	tablespoons canola oil
1	tablespoon lemon juice
1	garlic clove, minced
1	tablespoon sugar
1/2	teaspoon salt

In a large bowl, combine the first seven ingredients. In a jar with a tight-fitting lid, combine the picante sauce, oil, lemon juice, garlic, sugar and salt; shake well.

Pour over pasta mixture and toss to coat. Cover and refrigerate overnight. YIELD: 10 SERVINGS.

NUTRITION FACTS: 3/4 cup equals 133 calories, 3 g fat (trace saturated fat), 0 cholesterol, 301 mg sodium, 24 g carbohydrate, 3 g fiber, 3 g protein. DIABETIC EXCHANGES: 1 starch, 1 vegetable, 1/2 fat.

garlic brussels sprouts

These brussels sprouts are special enough for company. I like to serve them for Thanksgiving dinner. If you can't find fresh sprouts, try using frozen ones.
—Myra Innes, Auburn, Kansas

1-1/2	pounds fresh brussels sprouts
4	garlic cloves, chopped
2	teaspoons olive oil
3	teaspoons butter, *divided*
1/2	cup reduced-sodium chicken broth
1/4	teaspoon salt
1/8	teaspoon pepper

Cut an "X" in the core end of each brussels sprout; set aside. In a large saucepan, saute garlic in oil and 1 teaspoon butter for 2-3 minutes or until golden brown. Add reserved sprouts; toss to coat.

Stir in the broth, salt and pepper; cover and cook for 12-14 minutes or until sprouts are tender. Drain; add the remaining butter and toss until melted. YIELD: 6 SERVINGS.

NUTRITION FACTS: 2/3 cup equals 83 calories, 3 g fat (1 g saturated fat), 5 mg cholesterol, 198 mg sodium, 11 g carbohydrate, 4 g fiber, 4 g protein. DIABETIC EXCHANGES: 2 vegetable, 1/2 fat.

garden salad with lemon dressing

I lightened up a tangy salad dressing by replacing some of the oil with lemon juice. The revamped dressing lends a refreshing twist to mixed greens, tomatoes, pepper rings and cucumber slices.
—Martha Pollock, Oregonia, Ohio

8	cups torn salad greens
1	cup grape *or* cherry tomatoes
1	medium cucumber, sliced
1	large sweet yellow *or* green pepper, cut into rings
1/4	cup lemon juice
4	teaspoons honey
2	teaspoons minced chives
1	teaspoon ground mustard
1/2	teaspoon salt
1/4	teaspoon pepper
2	tablespoons olive *or* canola oil

In a large bowl, combine the salad greens, tomatoes, cucumber and pepper rings. In a small bowl, whisk the lemon juice, honey, chives, mustard, salt and pepper until blended. Gradually whisk in oil until dressing thickens. Drizzle over salad; toss to coat. YIELD: 4 SERVINGS.

NUTRITION FACTS: 2 cups equals 143 calories, 8 g fat (1 g saturated fat), 0 cholesterol, 328 mg sodium, 19 g carbohydrate, 5 g fiber, 4 g protein. DIABETIC EXCHANGES: 3 vegetable, 1-1/2 fat.

garden salad with lemon dressing

italian vegetable saute

italian vegetable saute (LF) (LC) (LS) (ML)

This speedy side dish is loaded with flavor. It's a wonderful way to use up garden bounty—the recipe was the result of an abundant crop of green peppers my parents grew.
—Kenda Nicholson, Honey Grove, Texas

2	medium green peppers, sliced
1	garlic clove, minced
1	teaspoon Italian seasoning
1	tablespoon butter
1	cup cherry tomatoes, halved
1/2	cup seasoned croutons, optional

In a skillet, saute the peppers, garlic and Italian seasoning in butter until peppers are crisp-tender, about 5 minutes. Add the tomatoes; cook for 1-2 minutes or until heated through. Sprinkle with the seasoned croutons if desired. **YIELD: 4 SERVINGS.**

NUTRITION FACTS: 1/2 cup (prepared without croutons) equals 47 calories, 3 g fat (2 g saturated fat), 8 mg cholesterol, 26 mg sodium, 5 g carbohydrate, 2 g fiber, 1 g protein. **DIABETIC EXCHANGES:** 1 vegetable, 1/2 fat.

vegetable slaw (LC) (ML)

We've nicknamed this crunchy salad "Christmas slaw" because of its pretty mix of red and green vegetables. But it's tasty any time. It's a great light lunch when stuffed into a whole wheat pita.
—Julie Copenhayer, Morganton, North Carolina

3	cups shredded cabbage
5	plum tomatoes, seeded and chopped
1	cup fresh broccoli florets, cut into small pieces
1	cup fresh cauliflowerets, cut into small pieces
1/2	cup chopped red onion

1/2	cup fat-free sour cream
1/4	cup reduced-fat mayonnaise
1	tablespoon cider vinegar
3/4	teaspoon salt
1/4	teaspoon pepper

In a large bowl, combine the cabbage, tomatoes, broccoli, cauliflower and onion.

In a small bowl, combine the sour cream, mayonnaise, vinegar, salt and pepper. Pour over cabbage mixture; toss to coat evenly. Cover and refrigerate until chilled. **YIELD: 6 SERVINGS.**

NUTRITIONAL FACTS: 3/4 cup equals 84 calories, 5 g fat (1 g saturated fat), 7 mg cholesterol, 402 mg sodium, 10 g carbohydrate, 3 g fiber, 3 g protein. **DIABETIC EXCHANGES:** 2 vegetable, 1 fat.

apple carrots (LC) (LS) (ML)

Glistening with a subtly sweet glaze, these nutritious carrots are sure to become a requested dish. Best of all, they take only minutes to cook in the microwave.
—Taste of Home Test Kitchen

2	pounds carrots, julienned
1/4	cup apple juice
1/4	cup butter
2	tablespoons brown sugar
1	teaspoon salt, optional
	Minced fresh parsley

In a 2-qt. microwave-safe casserole, combine carrots and apple juice. Cover and microwave on high for 6-8 minutes or until crisp-tender, stirring once. Add the butter, brown sugar and salt if desired; toss to coat. Sprinkle with parsley. **YIELD: 12 SERVINGS.**

NUTRITION FACTS: 1/2 cup (prepared without salt) equals 76 calories, 4 g fat (2 g saturated fat), 10 mg cholesterol, 80 mg sodium, 10 g carbohydrate, 2 g fiber, 1 g protein. **DIABETIC EXCHANGES:** 1 vegetable, 1 fat.

Editor's Note: *This recipe was tested in a 1,100-watt microwave.*

apple carrots

main dishes

teriyaki
pork page 74

turkey tomato pizza

turkey tomato pizza

My husband and I tried this pizza at a party, and I had to ask for the recipe. Now it's a hit at get-togethers at our house. Everyone loves the twist on ordinary pizza.
—Michelle Beall, Westminster, Maryland

1 tube (13.8 ounces) refrigerated pizza crust	1/4 pound thinly sliced deli turkey, julienned
2 teaspoons sesame seeds	3 bacon strips, cooked and crumbled
1/4 cup reduced-fat mayonnaise	2 small tomatoes, thinly sliced
1/4 teaspoon grated lemon peel	1 cup (4 ounces) shredded reduced-fat Swiss cheese
1 cup (4 ounces) shredded reduced-fat Mexican cheese blend	2 tablespoons thinly sliced green onions
1 teaspoon dried basil	

Unroll the pizza crust onto a 15-in. x 10-in. x 1-in. baking pan coated with cooking spray. Flatten dough and build up edges slightly. Prick dough several times with a fork; sprinkle with sesame seeds. Bake at 425° for 10-12 minutes or until lightly browned.

Combine the mayonnaise and lemon peel; spread over crust. Sprinkle with Mexican cheese and basil. Top with turkey, bacon, tomatoes and Swiss cheese. Bake for 7-9 minutes or until the crust is golden brown and cheese is melted. Sprinkle with onions. **YIELD: 6 SERVINGS.**

NUTRITION FACTS: 1 slice equals 284 calories, 11 g fat (4 g saturated fat), 27 mg cholesterol, 865 mg sodium, 27 g carbohydrate, 1 g fiber, 19 g protein. **DIABETIC EXCHANGES:** 2 meat, 1-1/2 starch, 1 vegetable, 1 fat.

Light
COOKING TIP

If you're trying to cut calories, opt for a thin pizza crust over a thick one. A pizza stone works well for a crispier crust and better browning. Before preheating the oven, place the stone on an oven rack in the lower third of the oven.

very veggie lasagna

apricot turkey stir-fry (LF)

Tender turkey, crunchy veggies and dried apricots make this simple stir-fry a standout. Try serving it over long-grain rice or whole-wheat pasta, too.
—Robin Chamberlin, La Costa, California

1	tablespoon cornstarch
1/2	cup apricot nectar
3	tablespoons reduced-sodium soy sauce
2	tablespoons white vinegar
1/4	teaspoon crushed red pepper flakes
1/2	cup dried apricot halves, cut in half lengthwise
1	pound turkey tenderloin, cut into thin slices
1	teaspoon canola oil
1	teaspoon sesame oil *or* additional canola oil
2-1/2	cups fresh snow peas
1	medium onion, chopped
1	medium sweet red *or* yellow pepper, cut into 1-inch pieces

Hot cooked couscous, optional

In a small bowl, combine the cornstarch, apricot nectar, soy sauce, vinegar and red pepper flakes until smooth. Add apricots; set aside.

In a large nonstick skillet or wok, stir-fry turkey in canola and sesame oil until no longer pink. Add the peas, onion and red pepper; stir-fry until crisp-tender. Remove meat and vegetables with a slotted spoon; keep warm.

Stir cornstarch mixture and gradually add to pan. Bring to a boil; cook and stir for 1-2 minutes or until thickened. Return meat and vegetables to the pan; toss to coat. Heat through. Serve with couscous if desired. **YIELD: 4 SERVINGS.**

NUTRITION FACTS: 1-1/2 cups stir-fry mixture, (calculated without the couscous) equals 270 calories, 3 g fat (1 g saturated fat), 82 mg cholesterol, 512 mg sodium, 27 g carbohydrate, 4 g fiber, 33 g protein. **DIABETIC EXCHANGES:** 4 very lean meat, 2 vegetable, 1 fruit, 1/2 fat.

very veggie lasagna (ML)

I created this quick and easy recipe to use up the abundance of fresh produce from my garden. This meatless version is a great way to get your daily dose of veggies while still enjoying the wonderful flavor and heartiness of lasagna.
—Bernice Baldwin, Glennie, Michigan

2	medium carrots, julienned
1	medium zucchini, cut into 1/4-inch slices
1	yellow summer squash, cut into 1/4-inch slices
1	medium onion, sliced
1	cup fresh broccoli florets
1/2	cup sliced celery
1/2	cup julienned sweet red pepper
1/2	cup julienned green pepper
2	garlic cloves, minced
1/2	to 1 teaspoon salt
2	tablespoons canola oil
1	jar (28 ounces) spaghetti sauce
14	lasagna noodles, cooked and drained
4	cups (16 ounces) shredded part-skim mozzarella cheese

In a large skillet, stir-fry the vegetables, garlic and salt in oil until crisp-tender.

Spread 3/4 cup spaghetti sauce in the greased 13-in. x 9-in. baking dish. Arrange seven noodles over sauce, overlapping as needed. Layer with half of the vegetables, spaghetti sauce and cheese. Repeat layers.

Cover and bake at 350° for 60-65 minutes or until bubbly. Let stand for 15 minutes before cutting. **YIELD: 12 SERVINGS.**

NUTRITION FACTS: 1 serving equals 295 calories, 11 g fat (5 g saturated fat), 23 mg cholesterol, 617 mg sodium, 34 g carbohydrate, 3 g fiber, 16 g protein. **DIABETIC EXCHANGES:** 1-1/2 fat, 1 starch, 1 vegetable, 1 reduced-fat milk.

apricot turkey stir-fry

asparagus chicken sandwiches

asparagus chicken sandwiches

These tasty open-faced sandwiches are a great way to use up leftover chicken or turkey. Served on toasted English muffins, slices of chicken and tomato are topped with fresh asparagus spears, then draped in a creamy lemon sauce.
—*Anca Cretan, Hagerstown, Maryland*

1	pound fresh asparagus, trimmed and cut into 3-inch pieces
1-1/2	cups reduced-fat sour cream
2	teaspoons lemon juice
1-1/2	teaspoons prepared mustard
1/2	teaspoon salt
8	ounces sliced cooked chicken breast
4	English muffins, split and toasted
2	medium tomatoes, sliced

Paprika, optional

In a large saucepan, bring 1/2 in. of water to a boil. Add asparagus; cover and boil for 3 minutes. Drain and immediately place asparagus in ice water. Drain and pat dry.

In the same pan, combine the sour cream, lemon juice, mustard and salt; cook on low until heated through. Remove from the heat.

Place chicken on a microwave-safe plate; microwave on high for 30-40 seconds or until warmed.

Place two English muffin halves on each serving plate. Top with the chicken, tomatoes, asparagus and sauce. Sprinkle with paprika if desired. **YIELD: 4 SERVINGS.**

NUTRITION FACTS: 2 topped muffin halves equals 385 calories, 11 g fat (7 g saturated fat), 78 mg cholesterol, 645 mg sodium, 40 g carbohydrate, 2 g fiber, 32 g protein. **DIABETIC EXCHANGES:** 2 starch, 2 lean meat, 1 vegetable, 1 fat, 1/2 reduced-fat milk.

Editor's Note: This recipe was tested in a 1,100-watt microwave.

vegetable steak stir-fry

Sirloin steak and tasty vegetables take center stage in this showstopper. While I don't have much time to cook, I do like to experiment with food. This quick dish is a favorite.
—*Pamela Brandal, Park City, Illinois*

3/4	pound boneless beef sirloin steak, cubed
3	teaspoons canola oil, *divided*
2	cups fresh broccoli florets
2	cups fresh cauliflowerets
2	cups julienned carrots
6	garlic cloves, minced
1	tablespoon cornstarch
3/4	cup beef broth
1/3	cup sherry *or* additional broth
1	tablespoon water
1-1/2	teaspoons soy sauce
1/4	teaspoon ground ginger
2	medium tomatoes, cut into wedges

Hot cooked rice, optional

In a large skillet or wok, stir-fry steak in 2 teaspoons oil until no longer pink. Remove and keep warm. In the same pan, heat the remaining oil. Add the broccoli, cauliflower, carrots and garlic; stir-fry until vegetables are crisp-tender.

In a small bowl, combine the cornstarch, broth, sherry or additional broth, water, soy sauce and ginger until smooth. Return beef to the pan. Stir cornstarch mixture and add to pan. Bring to a boil; cook and stir for 2 minutes or until thickened. Add tomatoes; heat through. Serve with rice if desired. **YIELD: 4 SERVINGS.**

NUTRITION FACTS: 1-cup serving (prepared with reduced-sodium soy sauce; calculated without rice) equals 251 calories, 9 g fat (2 g saturated fat), 50 mg cholesterol, 364 mg sodium, 18 g carbohydrate, 5 g fiber, 23 g protein. **DIABETIC EXCHANGES:** 3 lean meat, 3 vegetable, 1/2 fat.

vegetable steak stir-fry

garden primavera ⓂⓁ

I made several changes to the original recipe for this pasta and vegetable toss to better suit my family's tastes. With its pretty color and mouth-watering flavor, this nutrient-rich dish makes a great meatless main course.

—Ann Heinonen, Howell, Michigan

8	ounces uncooked fettuccine
1	cup fresh broccoli florets
1	medium sweet red pepper, julienned
1	medium carrot, sliced
1/2	cup sliced mushrooms
1/4	cup sliced celery
1	garlic clove, minced
1	tablespoon olive oil
3/4	cup V8 juice
1/4	cup minced fresh basil
1	cup frozen peas, thawed
1/2	teaspoon salt
1/8	teaspoon pepper
2	tablespoons shredded Parmesan cheese

Cook fettuccine according to package directions. Meanwhile, in a large nonstick skillet, saute the broccoli, red pepper, carrot, mushrooms, celery and garlic in oil for 3 minutes. Add V8 juice and basil; bring to a boil. Reduce heat; simmer, uncovered, for 3 minutes. Stir in the peas, salt and pepper; simmer 2 minutes longer or until peas are tender.

Drain fettuccine; add to vegetable mixture and toss to coat. Sprinkle with Parmesan cheese. **YIELD: 4 SERVINGS.**

NUTRITION FACTS: 1-1/2 cups equals 310 calories, 6 g fat (1 g saturated fat), 2 mg cholesterol, 529 mg sodium, 54 g carbohydrate, 6 g fiber, 12 g protein. **DIABETIC EXCHANGES:** 3 starch, 2 vegetable, 1 fat.

garden primavera

mushroom broccoli pizza ⓂⓁ

I'm not a vegetarian, but I do like meatless entrees. Since I have a green thumb, I make this delectable pizza with homegrown veggies from my garden. Using whole wheat flour for the crust adds fiber, and you can even add a little ground flaxseed for a bit of extra nutrition.

—Kathleen Kelley, Roseburg, Oregon

1	package (1/4 ounce) active dry yeast
3/4	cup warm water (110° to 115°)
1	teaspoon olive oil
1/2	teaspoon sugar
1/2	cup whole wheat flour
1/2	teaspoon salt
1-1/2	cups all-purpose flour

TOPPINGS:

3	cups broccoli florets
1	cup sliced fresh mushrooms
1/4	cup chopped onion
4	garlic cloves, minced
1	tablespoon olive oil
1/2	cup pizza sauce
4	plum tomatoes, sliced lengthwise
1/4	cup chopped fresh basil
1-1/2	cups (6 ounces) shredded part-skim mozzarella cheese
1/3	cup shredded Parmesan cheese

In a bowl, dissolve yeast in warm water. Add oil and sugar; mix well. Combine whole wheat flour and salt; stir into yeast mixture until smooth. Stir in enough all-purpose flour to form a soft dough.

Turn onto a floured surface; knead until smooth and elastic, about 6-8 minutes. Place in a bowl coated with cooking spray, turning once to coat top. Cover and let rise in a warm place until doubled, about 1-1/2 hours.

Punch dough down. Press onto the bottom and 1 in. up the sides of a 12-in. pizza pan coated with cooking spray. Prick dough several times with a fork. Bake crust at 425° for 6-8 minutes.

Place broccoli in a steamer basket; place in a saucepan over 1 in. of water. Bring to a boil; cover and steam for 5-6 minutes or until crisp-tender. Transfer broccoli to a colander. Rinse with cold water; drain and set aside.

In a nonstick skillet, saute mushrooms, onion and garlic in oil until mushrooms are tender. Spread pizza sauce over crust. Top with mushroom mixture, tomatoes, broccoli, basil and cheeses. Bake at 425° for 12-14 minutes or until crust is golden and cheese is melted. **YIELD: 6 SLICES.**

NUTRITION FACTS: 1 slice equals 283 calories, 9 g fat (4 g saturated fat), 19 mg cholesterol, 492 mg sodium, 39 g carbohydrate, 4 g fiber, 15 g protein. **DIABETIC EXCHANGES:** 2 starch, 2 lean meat, 1/2 fat.

pita burgers

pita burgers

I serve this tasty variation on the traditional hamburger at backyard get-togethers. Similar to Greek gyros, the herbed ground beef patties are stuffed in pita breads with a yummy cucumber-lettuce mixture.

—Dorothy Wiedeman, Eaton, Colorado

    1   small onion, chopped
    1   garlic clove, minced
    1   teaspoon dried oregano
  3/4   teaspoon salt
  1/2   teaspoon dried basil
  1/4   teaspoon dried rosemary, crushed
1-1/2   pounds lean ground beef
    2   cups shredded lettuce
    1   medium cucumber, seeded and chopped
    1   cup (8 ounces) reduced-fat plain yogurt
    1   tablespoon sesame seeds, toasted
    6   whole pita breads, halved

In a small bowl, combine the onion, garlic and seasonings; crumble beef over mixture and mix well. Shape mixture into six patties.

Grill or broil for 5-7 minutes on each side or until a meat thermometer reads 160° and juices run clear.

Meanwhile, in a small bowl, combine the lettuce, cucumber, yogurt and sesame seeds. Top each burger with lettuce mixture; serve on pitas. **YIELD: 6 SERVINGS.**

NUTRITION FACTS: 2 stuffed pita halves equals 409 calories, 12 g fat (5 g saturated fat), 44 mg cholesterol, 731 mg sodium, 40 g carbohydrate, 3 g fiber, 32 g protein. **DIABETIC EXCHANGES:** 3-1/2 lean meat, 2-1/2 starch, 1 fat.

marinated chicken breasts ⓛⓒ

Bring some international flair to your barbecues with this Indian-inspired marinade and basting sauce. If you're not in the mood for chicken, use turkey tenderloins instead.

—Linda Fisher, Columbus, Ohio

    1   teaspoon chicken bouillon granules
  1/2   cup warm apple juice
    1   cup white wine *or* chicken broth
    2   to 4 tablespoons olive oil
    1   to 2 tablespoons curry powder
    2   teaspoons celery salt
    2   teaspoons soy sauce
    1   garlic clove, peeled and sliced
    6   bone-in chicken breast halves (6 ounces *each*)

In a small bowl, dissolve bouillon in apple juice. Add the wine, oil, curry powder, celery salt, soy sauce and garlic. Pour 1 cup marinade into a large resealable plastic bag; add the chicken. Seal bag and turn to coat; refrigerate overnight. Cover and refrigerate remaining marinade.

Drain and discard marinade from chicken. Grill, covered, over medium heat for 35-40 minutes or until a meat thermometer reads 170°, turning and basting occasionally with reserved marinade. **YIELD: 6 SERVINGS.**

NUTRITION FACTS: 1 chicken breast (calculated with 2 tablespoons olive oil and chicken skin removed) equals 214 calories, 8 g fat (1 g saturated fat), 68 mg cholesterol, 364 mg sodium, 4 g carbohydrate, 0.55 g fiber, 25 g protein. **DIABETIC EXCHANGES:** 3 lean meat, 1 fat.

turkey avocado sandwiches

Jazz up a plain turkey sandwich with just-picked vegetables and fresh cilantro. The zesty taco and hot pepper sauces quickly kick the heat up a notch. Delicious and healthy, this sandwich can't be beat!

—Dave Bremson, Plantation, Florida

    3   ounces fat-free cream cheese
    2   teaspoons taco sauce
    4   drops hot pepper sauce
    4   slices whole wheat bread
    4   ounces sliced cooked turkey
  1/2   medium ripe avocado, peeled and sliced
    1   medium ripe tomato, sliced
    2   to 4 tablespoons minced fresh cilantro
    2   lettuce leaves

In a large bowl, beat cream cheese until smooth; beat in taco sauce and pepper sauce. Spread on each slice of bread.

Layer the turkey, avocado and tomato on two slices of bread; sprinkle with cilantro. Top with lettuce and remaining bread. **YIELD: 2 SERVINGS.**

NUTRITION FACTS: 1 sandwich equals 399 calories, 11 g fat (2 g saturated fat), 52 mg cholesterol, 617 mg sodium, 40 g carbohydrate, 7 g fiber, 33 g protein. **DIABETIC EXCHANGES:** 3 lean meat, 2 starch, 2 vegetable, 1/2 fat.

teriyaki pork

NUTRITION FACTS: 1-1/2 cups stir-fry mixture (calculated without rice) equals 302 calories, 11 g fat (3 g saturated fat), 63 mg cholesterol, 802 mg sodium, 20 g carbohydrate, 5 g fiber, 30 g protein. **DIABETIC EXCHANGES:** 3 lean meat, 3 vegetable, 1/2 starch, 1/2 fat.

turkey meat loaf LC

I created the recipe for this delicious meat loaf one evening when I was hurrying to start dinner and had just a few ingredients on hand. Using lean ground turkey is a great alternative to the traditional red-meat version.
—Tamie Foley, Thousand Oaks, California

2	egg whites
1/3	cup ketchup
1	tablespoon Worcestershire sauce
1	teaspoon dried basil
1/2	teaspoon salt
1/2	teaspoon pepper
1	small onion, grated
1	small potato, finely shredded
1	small sweet red pepper, finely chopped
2	pounds lean ground turkey

In a large bowl, whisk together the first six ingredients. Stir in onion, potato and red pepper. Crumble turkey over mixture and mix well. Shape into a 12-in. x 4-in. loaf in a foil-lined 13-in. x 9-in. baking pan.

Bake, uncovered, at 350° for 60-70 minutes or until meat is no longer pink and a meat thermometer reads 165°. **YIELD: 8 SERVINGS.**

NUTRITION FACTS: 1 serving equals 200 calories, 9 g fat (3 g saturated fat), 90 mg cholesterol, 409 mg sodium, 7 g carbohydrate, 1 g fiber, 21 g protein. **DIABETIC EXCHANGES:** 3 lean meat, 1 fat.

teriyaki pork

I season tender pork loin and an assortment of crisp-tender vegetables with soy sauce and garlic marinade to create this wonderfully savory stir-fry.
—Molly Gee, Plainwell, Michigan

3/4	cup reduced-sodium chicken broth, *divided*
1/3	cup reduced-sodium soy sauce
2	tablespoons red wine vinegar
2	teaspoons honey
2	teaspoons garlic powder
1	pound boneless pork loin chops, cut into thin strips
1	tablespoon canola oil
2	cups fresh broccoli florets
3	medium carrots, sliced
3	celery ribs, sliced
4	cups shredded cabbage
6	green onions, sliced
1	tablespoon cornstarch

Hot cooked rice, optional

In a small bowl, combine 1/4 cup broth, soy sauce, vinegar, honey and garlic powder. Pour 1/3 cup marinade into a large resealable plastic bag; add the pork. Seal bag and turn to coat; refrigerate for 1 hour. Cover and refrigerate remaining marinade.

Drain and discard marinade from pork. In large nonstick skillet or wok, stir-fry pork in oil for 2-3 minutes or until no longer pink. Remove and keep warm. In the same pan, stir-fry broccoli and carrots in reserved marinade for 2 minutes. Add celery; stir-fry for 2 minutes. Add cabbage and green onions; stir-fry 2-3 minutes longer or until vegetables are crisp-tender.

Combine cornstarch and remaining broth until smooth; stir into vegetable mixture. Bring to a boil; cook and stir until thickened. Return pork to the pan; heat through. Serve with rice if desired. **YIELD: 4 SERVINGS.**

turkey meat loaf

baked cod

In an ungreased 13-in. x 9-in. baking dish, combine hash browns, beans and carrots. Top with chicken. Combine remaining ingredients; pour over chicken and vegetables.

Cover and bake at 375° for 50 minutes. Uncover; bake 25-30 minutes longer or until a meat thermometer reads 170°. **YIELD: 4 SERVINGS.**

NUTRITION FACTS: 1 serving (prepared with skinless chicken breasts, reduced-fat reduced-sodium mushroom soup and reduced-sodium onion soup mix and without salt) equals 428 calories, 5 g fat (0 saturated fat), 73 mg cholesterol, 685 mg sodium, 62 g carbohydrate, 8 g fiber, 34 g protein. **DIABETIC EXCHANGES:** 3-1/2 starch, 3 very lean meat, 1 vegetable, 1/2 fat.

baked cod (lc)

These fish fillets are quick to fix...and they bake in no time! Brushed with ranch salad dressing and coated with seasoned stuffing crumbs and parsley, the cod fillets are moist and flavorful. Our home economists sized the recipe to feed just two.
—Taste of Home Test Kitchen

1	cup seasoned stuffing croutons, crushed
1	tablespoon minced fresh parsley
2	cod fillets (6 ounces *each*)
1	tablespoon reduced-fat ranch salad dressing

Refrigerated butter-flavored spray

In a shallow bowl, combine the crushed croutons and parsley. Drizzle cod with salad dressing, then coat with crumb mixture. Spritz with butter-flavored spray.

Place in an 11-in. x 7-in. baking dish coated with cooking spray. Bake, uncovered, at 400° for 10-15 minutes or until fish flakes easily with a fork. **YIELD: 2 SERVINGS.**

NUTRITION FACTS: 1 fillet equals 244 calories, 5 g fat (1 g saturated fat), 75 mg cholesterol, 423 mg sodium, 15 g carbohydrate, 1 g fiber, 33 g protein. **DIABETIC EXCHANGES:** 4 very lean meat, 1 starch, 1/2 fat.

chicken meal-in-one

This entree is perfect for busy moms who want to prepare a wholesome meal but don't have much time to slave in the kitchen. I can assemble this dinner-in-a-dish in just 10 minutes and then pop it in the oven.
—Jina Nickel, Lawton, Oklahoma

4-1/2	cups frozen shredded hash brown potatoes
2	cups frozen cut green beans, thawed
1	cup frozen sliced carrots, thawed
4	bone-in chicken breasts (6 ounces *each*)
1	can (10-3/4 ounces) condensed cream of chicken *or* mushroom soup, undiluted
3/4	cup water
2	tablespoons onion soup mix

Salt and pepper to taste

chuck wagon wraps

If you're a fan of baked beans, you'll love this robust wrap. I mix the beans with beef, corn and cheese, then roll it all up in tortillas. This mixture works great for lettuce wraps, too.
—Wendy Conger, Winfield, Illinois

1	pound lean ground beef
1	can (28 ounces) barbecue-flavored baked beans
2	cups frozen corn, thawed
4-1/2	teaspoons Worcestershire sauce
1	cup (4 ounces) shredded reduced-fat cheddar cheese
12	flour tortillas (8 inches), warmed
3	cups shredded lettuce
1-1/2	cups chopped fresh tomatoes
3/4	cup reduced-fat sour cream

In a large nonstick skillet, cook beef over medium heat until no longer pink; drain. Stir in beans, corn and Worcestershire sauce; mix well. Bring to a boil. Reduce heat; simmer, uncovered, for 4-5 minutes or until heated through. Sprinkle with cheese; cook 1-2 minutes longer.

Spoon about 1/2 cup of mixture off center on each tortilla; top with lettuce, tomatoes and sour cream. Roll up. **YIELD: 12 SERVINGS.**

NUTRITION FACTS: 1 wrap equals 373 calories, 11 g fat (4 g saturated fat), 27 mg cholesterol, 605 mg sodium, 50 g carbohydrate, 4 g fiber, 20 g protein. **DIABETIC EXCHANGES:** 3 starch, 2 lean meat, 1/2 fat.

chuck wagon wraps

chicken lasagna

For a cooking class several years ago, I lightened up a classic lasagna recipe and created this chicken version. It was preferred over the traditional dish in taste tests in my class and by my family and friends as well.

—Dena Stapelman, Laurel, Nebraska

10	uncooked lasagna noodles
1	pound boneless skinless chicken breasts
1	can (14-1/2 ounces) diced tomatoes, undrained
1	can (12 ounces) tomato paste
1-1/2	cups sliced fresh mushrooms
1/4	cup chopped onion
1	tablespoon dried basil
1-3/4	teaspoons salt, *divided*
1/8	teaspoon garlic powder
3	cups (24 ounces) 2% cottage cheese
1/2	cup egg substitute
1/2	cup grated Parmesan cheese
1/3	cup minced fresh parsley
1/2	teaspoon pepper
2	cups (8 ounces) shredded part-skim mozzarella cheese

Cook noodles according to package directions. Meanwhile, broil chicken 6 in. from the heat until juices run clear; let stand for 15 minutes or until cool enough to handle. Shred chicken with two forks. Drain noodles; set aside.

In a large nonstick skillet, combine the shredded chicken, tomatoes, tomato paste, mushrooms, onion, basil, 3/4 teaspoon salt and garlic powder. Bring to a boil. Reduce heat; cover and simmer for 25-30 minutes. In a bowl, combine the cottage cheese, egg substitute, Parmesan cheese, parsley, pepper and remaining salt.

In a 13-in. x 9-in. baking dish coated with cooking spray, place half of the noodles, overlapping them. Layer with half of the cheese mixture, chicken mixture and mozzarella. Repeat layers. Cover and bake at 375° for 25-30 minutes or until bubbly. Uncover; bake 5 minutes longer. Let stand for 15 minutes before cutting. YIELD: 12 SERVINGS.

NUTRITION FACTS: 1 serving equals 240 calories, 7 g fat (4 g saturated fat), 43 mg cholesterol, 1,038 mg sodium, 17 g carbohydrate, 2 g fiber, 28 g protein. DIABETIC EXCHANGES: 2 lean meat, 1 starch, 1 fat.

ziti alfredo with vegetables

A creamy dressing, lots of flavor and an unexpected hint of nutmeg make this hearty pasta dish so delicious. The recipe calls for an entire package of spinach so I know my family is getting plenty of folate, beta-carotene and vitamin K.

—Emma Magielda, Amsterdam, New York

1	medium onion, chopped
2	garlic cloves, minced
2	teaspoons olive oil
8	ounces uncooked ziti *or* small tube pasta
2	tablespoons butter
3	tablespoons all-purpose flour
1	cup fat-free milk
1-1/2	cups fat-free half-and-half
1	cup shredded Parmesan cheese
2	teaspoons Italian seasoning
1/4	teaspoon salt

Dash white pepper

Dash ground nutmeg

1	can (14-1/2 ounces) Italian diced tomatoes, drained
1	package (10 ounces) frozen chopped spinach, thawed and squeezed dry

In a small saucepan, saute onion and garlic in oil until tender; set aside. Cook ziti according to package directions. Meanwhile, in a large saucepan, melt butter; stir in flour until smooth. Reduce heat; slowly add milk.

Stir in half-and-half. Bring to a boil over medium-low heat; cook and stir for 2 minutes or until thickened. Reduce heat; add the Parmesan cheese, Italian seasoning, salt, pepper and nutmeg. Stir until cheese is melted.

Add the tomatoes, spinach and onion mixture; heat through. Drain the ziti; toss with vegetable mixture. YIELD: 8 SERVINGS.

NUTRITION FACTS: 1 cup equals 264 calories, 8 g fat (4 g saturated fat), 16 mg cholesterol, 488 mg sodium, 35 g carbohydrate, 3 g fiber, 13 g protein. DIABETIC EXCHANGES: 1-1/2 starch, 1-1/2 fat, 1 vegetable, 1/2 fat-free milk.

chicken lasagna

greek hero

greek hero ⓜ

With plenty of garden-fresh flavors and a robust bean spread that packs protein, this stacked submarine makes a satisfying meal-in-one for lunch or dinner.
—Margaret Wilson, Hemet, California

HUMMUS:

  2 tablespoons lemon juice
  1 tablespoon olive oil
  1 can (15 ounces) garbanzo beans *or* chickpeas, rinsed and drained
  2 garlic cloves, minced
  1 teaspoon dried oregano
1/4 teaspoon salt
1/8 teaspoon pepper

SANDWICH:

  1 loaf (8 ounces) unsliced French bread
  2 medium sweet red peppers, cut into thin strips
1/2 medium cucumber, sliced
  2 small tomatoes, sliced
1/4 cup thinly sliced red onion
1/4 cup chopped ripe olives
1/4 cup chopped pimiento-stuffed olives
1/2 cup crumbled feta cheese
  4 lettuce leaves

For hummus, in a food processor, combine the lemon juice, oil and beans; cover and process until smooth. Stir in the garlic, oregano, salt and pepper.

Slice bread in half horizontally. Carefully hollow out bottom half, leaving a 1/2-in. shell. Spread hummus into shell. Layer with the red peppers, cucumber, tomatoes, onion, olives, cheese and lettuce. Replace bread top. Cut into four portions. YIELD: 4 SERVINGS.

NUTRITION FACTS: 1 serving equals 350 calories, 12 g fat (4 g saturated fat), 17 mg cholesterol, 1,219 mg sodium, 50 g carbohydrate, 9 g fiber, 12 g protein. DIABETIC EXCHANGES: 2-1/2 starch, 2 vegetable, 1-1/2 fat, 1 lean meat.

rosemary chicken ⓛ ⓛ

A fast-to-fix overnight marinade with dried rosemary gives wonderful essence flavor to this tender chicken.
—Marcia Morgan, Chevy Chase, Maryland

  1 cup orange juice
1/4 cup olive oil
  3 garlic cloves, minced
  1 tablespoon dried rosemary, crushed
  1 tablespoon dried thyme
  8 boneless skinless chicken breast halves (4 ounces *each*)

Combine the first five ingredients; pour half into a large resealable plastic bag; add chicken. seal bag and turn to coat. Refrigerate for 8 hours or overnight. Cover and refrigerate reserved marinade for basting.

Drain and discard marinade. Grill chicken, uncovered, over medium heat or broil 4 in. from the heat for 3 minutes on each side. Baste with reserved marinade. Continue cooking for 6-8 minutes or until a meat thermometer reads 170°. YIELD: 8 SERVINGS.

NUTRITION FACTS: 1 chicken breast half equals 200 calories, 8 g fat (0 saturated fat), 73 mg cholesterol, 64 mg sodium, 3 g carbohydrate, 0 fiber, 27 g protein. DIABETIC EXCHANGES: 4 very lean meat, 1 fat.

veggie-topped fillets ⓛ

These easy-to-prepare sole fillets are baked in a mild tomato-based sauce. Best of all, they have under 200 calories.
—Joan Shirley, Trego, Montana

    4 sole *or* walleye fillets (6 ounces *each*)
  3/4 teaspoon salt, *divided*
  1/8 teaspoon pepper
1-1/2 cups V8 juice
  1/2 cup chopped celery
  1/2 cup chopped onion
  1/4 cup chopped green pepper
    1 tablespoon lemon juice
    1 teaspoon sugar
    1 tablespoon butter

Hot cooked rice, optional

Place fillets in a 13-in. x 9-in. baking dish coated with cooking spray; sprinkle with 1/2 teaspoon salt and pepper. In a saucepan, combine the V8 juice, celery, onion, green pepper, lemon juice, sugar and remaining salt; bring to a boil. Cook over medium-low heat for 5-6 minutes or until vegetables are tender. Pour over fish; dot with butter.

Bake, uncovered, at 350° for 10-15 minutes or until fish flakes easily with a fork. Serve with rice if desired. YIELD: 4 SERVINGS.

NUTRITION FACTS: 1 fillet with 1/2 cup sauce (calculated without rice) equals 199 calories, 5 g fat (2 g saturated fat), 88 mg cholesterol, 779 mg sodium, 8 g carbohydrate, 1 g fiber, 29 g protein. DIABETIC EXCHANGES: 4 very lean meat, 1 vegetable, 1/2 fat.

asian steak skewers

asian steak skewers

I'm always on the lookout for light meals that will satisfy my family, and these stuffed kabobs fit the bill. Served with a creamy mustard sauce, the colorful bundles are special enough for company.

—Gina Hatchell, Mickleton, New Jersey

1	pound beef sirloin tip roast
1/3	cup reduced-sodium soy sauce
1/4	cup sugar
1/2	teaspoon ground ginger
1	cup water
4	medium carrots, julienned
1/2	pound fresh green beans, trimmed
1	large sweet red pepper, julienned
1/2	cup reduced-fat sour cream
2	tablespoons Dijon mustard
1-1/4	teaspoons prepared horseradish

Cut beef widthwise into 16 slices, 1/4 in. thick. In a large resealable plastic bag, combine the soy sauce, sugar and ginger; add beef. Seal bag and turn to coat; refrigerate for 4 hours.

In a large saucepan, bring water and carrots to a boil. Reduce heat; cover and simmer for 3 minutes. Add the beans and red pepper; cover and simmer for 3-5 minutes or until vegetables are crisp-tender. Drain and immediately place vegetables in ice water. Drain and pat dry.

Drain and discard marinade from beef. Arrange three beans, one carrot strip and one pepper strip down the center of each beef slice; roll up. For each kabob, use metal or soaked wooden skewers and thread two bundles on two parallel skewers.

If grilling the kabobs, coat grill rack with cooking spray before starting the grill. Grill kabobs, covered, over medium heat or broil 4-6 in. from the heat for 3-5 minutes on each side or until beef reaches desired doneness.

In a small bowl, combine the sour cream, mustard and horseradish. Serve with kabobs. **YIELD: 4 SERVINGS.**

NUTRITION FACTS: 4 bundles with 2 tablespoons sauce equals 304 calories, 10 g fat (5 g saturated fat), 87 mg cholesterol, 542 mg sodium, 21 g carbohydrate, 5 g fiber, 31 g protein. **DIABETIC EXCHANGES:** 4 lean meat, 3 vegetable, 1/2 fat.

tasty lentil tacos ⓜ

When my husband's cholesterol numbers rose, I quickly lowered the fat in our family's diet. Finding dishes that were healthy for him and yummy for our five children was a challenge. This fun taco recipe was a huge hit with everyone.

—Michelle Thomas, Bangor, Maine

1	cup finely chopped onion
1	garlic clove, minced
1	teaspoon canola oil
1	cup dried lentils, rinsed
1	tablespoon chili powder
2	teaspoons ground cumin
1	teaspoon dried oregano
2-1/2	cups chicken or vegetable broth
1	cup salsa
12	taco shells
1-1/2	cups shredded lettuce
1	cup chopped fresh tomato
1-1/2	cups (6 ounces) shredded reduced-fat cheddar cheese
6	tablespoons fat-free sour cream

In a large nonstick skillet, saute the onion and garlic in oil until tender. Add the lentils, chili powder, cumin and oregano; cook and stir for 1 minute. Add broth; bring to a boil. Reduce heat; cover and simmer for 25-30 minutes or until the lentils are tender.

Uncover; cook for 6-8 minutes or until mixture is thickened. Mash lentils slightly. Stir in salsa.

Spoon about 1/4 cup lentil mixture into each taco shell. Top with lettuce, tomato, cheese and sour cream. **YIELD: 6 SERVINGS.**

NUTRITION FACTS: 2 tacos equals 401 calories, 16 g fat (7 g saturated fat), 33 mg cholesterol, 973 mg sodium, 43 g carbohydrate, 14 g fiber, 24 g protein. **DIABETIC EXCHANGES:** 2-1/2 lean meat, 2 starch, 1-1/2 fat.

tasty lentil tacos

salmon with orange-kiwi salsa

My husband is a meat-and-potatoes kind of guy, so when he raved about this wonderful marinated baked salmon at a dinner party, I knew I had to have the recipe. The citrusy salsa is as pretty as it is tasty.
—Maria Davis, Flower Mound, Texas

1	cup white wine *or* chicken broth
1	cup white grapefruit juice
8	garlic cloves, minced
1	teaspoon dill weed
4	salmon fillets (6 ounces *each*)

SALSA:

1	cup chopped orange
1	cup chopped kiwifruit
1	large onion, chopped
1	jalapeno pepper, seeded and diced

In a small bowl, combine the first four ingredients. Pour half into a large resealable plastic bag; add salmon. Seal bag and turn to coat; refrigerate for 2 hours. Cover and refrigerate remaining marinade. In a small bowl, combine salsa ingredients. Cover and refrigerate until serving.

Drain and discard marinade from fish. Place salmon in a 13-in. x 9-in. baking dish. Pour reserved marinade over salmon. Cover and bake at 375° for 20-25 minutes or until fish flakes easily with a fork. Serve fillets with salsa. **YIELD: 4 SERVINGS.**

NUTRITION FACTS: 1 fillet with 1/2 cup salsa equals 294 calories, 7 g fat (2 g saturated fat), 80 mg cholesterol, 90 mg sodium, 21 g carbohydrate, 3 g fiber, 36 g protein. **DIABETIC EXCHANGES:** 5 very lean meat, 1 fruit, 1 vegetable, 1 fat.

Editor's Note: When cutting hot peppers, disposable gloves are recommended. Avoid touching your face.

Light
COOKING TIP

Boost your daily intake of omega-3 with fresh seafood, including salmon, tuna and mackerel. Eggs and milk are also good sources. Another easy trick is to sprinkle ground flaxseed on cereal or salads, or substitute flaxseed oil for other oils.

makeover loaded pizza

makeover loaded pizza

With ingredients from all four food groups, this guilt-free pizza doesn't skimp on nutrition. It's comfort food at its best!
—Taste of Home Test Kitchen

1-1/2	cups sliced fresh mushrooms
1/4	cup *each* chopped green pepper, sweet red pepper, white onion and red onion
2	garlic cloves, minced
1	tablespoon canola oil
1/4	pound lean ground beef
1	turkey Italian sausage link (4 ounces), casing removed
2	teaspoons cornmeal
1	loaf (1 pound) frozen bread dough, thawed
1	can (8 ounces) tomato sauce
2	tablespoons minced fresh parsley
2	teaspoons Italian seasoning
1/4	teaspoon garlic powder
1/8	teaspoon pepper
15	turkey pepperoni slices (1 ounce)
2	tablespoons sliced ripe olives
1-1/4	cups shredded part-skim mozzarella cheese
1/4	cup shredded reduced-fat cheddar cheese

In a nonstick skillet, saute the mushrooms, peppers, onions and garlic in oil until tender; remove and set aside. In the same skillet, cook beef and sausage over medium heat until no longer pink; drain.

Coat a 14-in. pizza pan with cooking spray and sprinkle with cornmeal. On a lightly floured surface, roll dough into a 15-in. circle.

Transfer to prepared pan. Build up edges slightly; prick dough thoroughly with a fork. Bake at 400° for 8-10 minutes or until lightly browned.

In a large bowl, combine the tomato sauce, parsley, Italian seasoning, garlic powder and pepper; spread over crust. Top with the vegetables, meat mixture, pepperoni and olives. Sprinkle with cheeses.

Bake for 8-10 minutes or until crust is golden and cheese is melted. **YIELD: 8 SERVINGS.**

NUTRITION FACTS: 1 slice equals 300 calories, 11 g fat (3 g saturated fat), 27 mg cholesterol, 758 mg sodium, 36 g carbohydrate, 3 g fiber, 18 g protein. **DIABETIC EXCHANGES:** 2 starch, 1 lean meat, 1 vegetable, 1 fat.

chicken and asparagus bundles (LC)

My husband is a big asparagus fan, so I had to try this recipe. It's a mainstay when I want something different but simple for guests. For variety, you can leave off the sauce and serve the bundles chilled for lunch.

—Donna Lohnes, Wooster, Ohio

4	boneless skinless chicken breast halves (4 ounces *each*)
20	fresh asparagus spears (about 1 pound), trimmed
4-1/2	teaspoons olive oil
2	teaspoons lemon juice
1/2	teaspoon dried basil
1/4	teaspoon dried thyme
1/4	teaspoon pepper
1/8	teaspoon salt
1/4	cup chopped green onions
2	teaspoons cornstarch
1	cup chicken broth

Flatten chicken breasts to 1/2 in. Wrap each around five asparagus spears; secure with toothpicks. Place in a 13-in. x 9-in. baking dish coated with cooking spray. Combine the oil, lemon juice and seasonings; pour over bundles. Cover asparagus tips with foil.

Cover and bake at 350° for 15 minutes. Uncover; sprinkle with the onions. Bake 12-15 minutes longer or until chicken is no longer pink and asparagus is crisp-tender. Remove bundles to a serving platter and keep warm.

needs longer in oven

In a small saucepan, combine cornstarch and broth until smooth; stir in pan juices. Bring to a boil; cook and stir for 2 minutes or until thickened. Remove toothpicks. Serve with sauce. **YIELD: 4 SERVINGS.**

NUTRITION FACTS: 1 bundle with about 1/3 sauce equals 207 calories, 7 g fat (1 g saturated fat), 66 mg cholesterol, 316 mg sodium, 6 g carbohydrate, 2 g fiber, 29 g protein. **DIABETIC EXCHANGES:** 3 lean meat, 1 vegetable, 1 fat.

chicken and asparagus bundles

lemon turkey burgers

lemon turkey burgers

My mom used to cook these juicy burgers in butter or a little bacon fat. I do all of my sauteing in olive oil or nonstick cooking spray, yet my lemon turkey burgers taste just as delicious as Mom's did.

—Jane Harris, Framingham, Massachusetts

1	egg, lightly beaten
1/3	cup finely chopped onion
3	tablespoons minced fresh parsley
2	tablespoons lemon juice
1	tablespoon grated lemon peel
3	garlic cloves, minced
1	teaspoon caraway seeds, crushed
1	teaspoon salt
1/2	teaspoon pepper
1	pound lean ground turkey
1	tablespoon olive oil
6	whole wheat sandwich rolls, split
6	lettuce leaves
6	thin tomato slices

In a large bowl, combine the first nine ingredients. Crumble turkey over mixture and mix well. Shape mixture into six patties.

In a large nonstick skillet, cook patties in oil in two batches over medium heat until a meat thermometer reaches 165° and juices run clear. Serve on rolls with lettuce and tomato. **YIELD: 6 SERVINGS.**

NUTRITION FACTS: 1 sandwich equals 268 calories, 11 g fat (3 g saturated fat), 95 mg cholesterol, 680 mg sodium, 24 g carbohydrate, 4 g fiber, 18 g protein. **DIABETIC EXCHANGES:** 2 lean meat, 1-1/2 starch, 1/2 fat.

savory spinach chicken roll-ups ⓛⓒ

The herb-flavored chicken stays tender and moist in this entree developed by our home economists.
—*Taste of Home Test Kitchen*

1	package (10 ounces) fresh spinach
1/4	cup chopped fresh mushrooms
1	green onion, finely chopped
1	to 2 garlic cloves, minced
2	teaspoons olive oil
1	egg, lightly beaten
1/4	cup crumbled feta cheese
1/4	cup dry bread crumbs
3/4	teaspoon dried rosemary, crushed, *divided*
1/4	teaspoon salt
4	boneless skinless chicken breast halves (1 pound)
1/2	teaspoon *each* dried basil and dried thyme
1/4	teaspoon pepper

In a large saucepan, place spinach in a steamer basket over 1 in. of boiling water. Cover and steam for 2-3 minutes or just until wilted. When cool enough to handle, squeeze spinach dry and finely chop.

In a nonstick skillet, saute the mushrooms, onion and garlic in oil until tender. Add the spinach; cook and stir for 2 minutes. Transfer to a large bowl. Stir in the egg, feta cheese, bread crumbs, 1/4 teaspoon rosemary and salt until well blended.

Flatten chicken to 1/4-in. thickness. Combine the basil, thyme, pepper and remaining rosemary; rub over one side of chicken. Spread spinach mixture over plain side; roll up. Secure with toothpicks.

In a large saucepan, place roll-ups in a steamer basket over 1 in. of boiling water. Cover and steam for 12-15 minutes or until chicken is no longer pink. **YIELD: 4 SERVINGS.**

NUTRITION FACTS: 1 roll-up equals 235 calories, 8 g fat (3 g saturated fat), 127 mg cholesterol, 456 mg sodium, 9 g carbohydrate, 2 g fiber, 32 g protein. **DIABETIC EXCHANGES:** 3 lean meat, 1 vegetable, 1 fat.

jambalaya

Unlike some versions, this quick-to-cook jambalaya doesn't have to simmer for hours. Jalapeno and cayenne pepper add some zip to the shrimp and chicken. Folks who like their food a bit spicy are sure to enjoy it.
—*Betty May, Topeka, Kansas*

1/2	pound boneless skinless chicken breasts, cut into 1-inch pieces
1	large onion, chopped
3/4	cup chopped green pepper
1	celery rib, chopped
2	jalapeno peppers, seeded and finely chopped
2	garlic cloves, minced
1	tablespoon canola oil
2	cans (14-1/2 ounces *each*) diced tomatoes, undrained
1/2	cup water
1	teaspoon dried thyme
1/2	teaspoon salt
1/4	teaspoon pepper
1/8	to 1/4 teaspoon cayenne pepper
1	pound uncooked medium shrimp, peeled and deveined
2	cups cooked long grain rice

In a large Dutch oven or saucepan, saute the chicken, onion, green pepper, celery, jalapenos and garlic in oil until chicken is no longer pink. Add the tomatoes, water, thyme, salt, pepper and cayenne; bring to a boil.

Reduce heat; cover and simmer for 15 minutes. Add shrimp; simmer 6-8 minutes longer or until shrimp turn pink. Stir in rice. **YIELD: 6 SERVINGS.**

NUTRITION FACTS: 1-1/2 cups equals 229 calories, 4 g fat (1 g saturated fat), 112 mg cholesterol, 502 mg sodium, 27 g carbohydrate, 4 g fiber, 21 g protein. **DIABETIC EXCHANGES:** 3 very lean meat, 2 vegetable, 1 starch, 1/2 fat.

Editor's Note: *When cutting hot peppers, disposable gloves are recommended. Avoid touching your face.*

jambalaya

southwestern skewers

southwestern skewers ⒧Ⓒ

Juicy chicken, cherry tomatoes, whole mushrooms and sweet peppers make these skewers filling. But it's the fresh garlic, chili powder, cumin and cayenne pepper that always give a truly zesty kick.

—Larry Smith, Youngstown, Ohio

1	bottle (8 ounces) reduced-fat Italian salad dressing
10	garlic cloves, minced
1	teaspoon white pepper
1	teaspoon chili powder
1	teaspoon ground cumin
1	teaspoon paprika
1/2	teaspoon cayenne pepper
1	medium green pepper, cut into 1-inch pieces
1	medium sweet red pepper, cut into 1-inch pieces
1	medium onion, cut into 1-inch pieces
8	large fresh mushrooms
8	cherry tomatoes
1	pound boneless skinless chicken breasts, cut into 1-inch cubes

In a large bowl, combine the first seven ingredients. Pour half into a large resealable plastic bag; add the vegetables. Seal bag and turn to coat. Pour remaining marinade into another large resealable plastic bag; add the chicken. Seal bag and turn to coat. Refrigerate vegetables and chicken for at least 2-3 hours.

If grilling the kabobs, coat grill rack with cooking spray before starting the grill. Drain chicken, discarding marinade. Drain vegetables, reserving marinade for basting.

On eight metal or soaked wooden skewers, alternately thread chicken and vegetables. Grill, covered, over medium heat or broil 4-6 in. from the heat for 6-8 minutes on each side or until chicken is no longer pink and vegetables are tender, basting frequently with reserved marinade. YIELD: 4 SERVINGS.

NUTRITION FACTS: 2 kabobs equals 231 calories, 7 g fat (1 g saturated fat), 63 mg cholesterol, 275 mg sodium, 15 g carbohydrate, 3 g fiber, 26 g protein. DIABETIC EXCHANGES: 3 lean meat, 2 vegetable, 1 fat.

vegetable lo mein ⓂⓁ

Crisp-tender veggies and soy sauce combine with linguine noodles in this colorful dish. It's great for lunch or even a light supper. Add tofu if you want to pack in a little extra protein.

—Sara Tatham, Plymouth, New Hampshire

6	ounces uncooked linguine
1	teaspoon cornstarch
1/2	vegetable bouillon cube
1/2	cup water
1/4	cup reduced-sodium soy sauce
1/2	pound fresh mushrooms, quartered
2	tablespoons canola oil, *divided*
1/2	pound fresh snow peas
8	green onions, sliced
4	celery ribs with leaves, sliced
1	large sweet red pepper, thinly sliced
1	can (14 ounces) bean sprouts, rinsed and drained

Cook pasta according to package directions; drain and set aside. In a small bowl, combine the cornstarch and bouillon; stir in the water and soy sauce and set aside.

In a nonstick skillet, stir-fry mushrooms in 1 tablespoon oil for 3 minutes or until tender; remove and keep warm. In same pan, heat remaining oil. Add remaining vegetables; stir-fry for 5 minutes or until crisp-tender.

Stir soy sauce mixture; add to pan. Bring to a boil; cook and stir for 2 minutes or until thickened. Add pasta and mushrooms. Heat through. YIELD: 4 SERVINGS.

NUTRITION FACTS: 1-1/2 cups equals 327 calories, 8 g fat (1 g saturated fat), 0.55 mg cholesterol, 1,081 mg sodium, 50 g carbohydrate, 7 g fiber, 12 g protein. DIABETIC EXCHANGES: 3 vegetable, 2 starch, 1-1/2 fat.

Editor's Note: This recipe was prepared with Knorr vegetable bouillon. A half-cube makes 1 cup prepared bouillon.

Light COOKING TIP

This Asian-inspired dish features a half pound of vitamin-rich snow peas, which are most flavorful and nutritious in early spring. In fact, snow peas are so named because there is often still snow on the ground when they are harvested.

pepperoni pizza supreme

Here's my in-a-hurry homemade alternative to typical restaurant pizza. Our family loves the crispy combination of vegetables and the lighter cheeses and turkey pepperoni. The only thing missing is the guilt!

—Sandy Schnack, Blue Springs, Missouri

1	prebaked thin Italian bread shell crust (10 ounces)
1	can (8 ounces) pizza sauce
1	tablespoon grated Parmesan cheese
1	teaspoon Italian seasoning
1/2	teaspoon garlic powder
1/2	cup sliced fresh mushrooms
1/2	cup chopped fresh broccoli florets
1/4	cup chopped green pepper
1/4	cup chopped sweet red pepper
1/2	cup shredded reduced-fat cheddar cheese
38	slices turkey pepperoni
1	cup (4 ounces) shredded part-skim mozzarella cheese

Place crust on an ungreased baking sheet. Spread with pizza sauce; sprinkle with the Parmesan cheese, Italian seasoning and garlic powder. Top with the mushrooms, broccoli and peppers.

Sprinkle with cheddar cheese. Top with pepperoni and mozzarella cheese. Bake at 400° for 14-18 minutes or until the vegetables are crisp-tender and the cheese is melted. **YIELD: 6 SLICES.**

NUTRITION FACTS: 1 slice equals 244 calories, 9 g fat (3 g saturated fat), 28 mg cholesterol, 698 mg sodium, 26 g carbohydrate, 1 g fiber, 17 g protein. **DIABETIC EXCHANGES:** 1-1/2 starch, 1-1/2 lean meat, 1 fat.

pepperoni pizza supreme

makeover chicken a la king casserole

makeover chicken a la king casserole

The traditional version of this rich, creamy casserole is a hearty crowd-pleaser but serves up a lot of fat and calories, too. Our home economists dish up this classic with more than 50% less fat and sodium and more than 75% less saturated fat, yet keep all the comfort you'd expect.

—Taste of Home Test Kitchen

8	ounces uncooked wide egg noodles
1	can (10-3/4 ounces) reduced-fat reduced-sodium condensed cream of chicken soup, undiluted
2/3	cup fat-free evaporated milk
6	ounces cubed reduced-fat process cheese (Velveeta)
2	cups cubed cooked chicken breast
1	cup sliced celery
1/4	cup chopped green pepper
1	jar (2 ounces) diced pimientos, drained
1/3	cup dry bread crumbs
1	tablespoon butter, melted
1/4	cup slivered almonds

Cook noodles according to package directions. Meanwhile, in a large saucepan, combine the soup and milk. Cook and stir over medium heat for 2 minutes. Reduce heat; stir in cheese until melted. Add the chicken, celery, green pepper and pimientos.

Drain noodles; add to chicken mixture and mix well. Transfer to a shallow 2-qt. baking dish coated with cooking spray. Cover and bake at 400° for 20 minutes.

Toss bread crumbs and butter; sprinkle over the top. Sprinkle with almonds. Bake, uncovered, for 10-15 minutes or until heated through and golden. **YIELD: 8 SERVINGS.**

NUTRITION FACTS: 1 cup equals 306 calories, 9 g fat (3 g saturated fat), 72 mg cholesterol, 405 mg sodium, 31 g carbohydrate, 2 g fiber, 24 g protein. **DIABETIC EXCHANGES:** 2 starch, 2 lean meat, 1 fat.

zucchini beef lasagna

This fresh-tasting and mildly seasoned Italian entree is a real crowd-pleaser.
—Brenda Tumasone, Newhall, California

1	pound lean ground beef
2	garlic cloves, minced
2	cans (8 ounces *each*) no-salt-added tomato sauce
1/2	cup water
1	can (6 ounces) tomato paste
2	bay leaves
1	teaspoon minced fresh parsley
1	teaspoon Italian seasoning
1	package (16 ounces) lasagna noodles, cooked, rinsed and drained
1	cup (8 ounces) fat-free cottage cheese
1	small zucchini, sliced and cooked
1	cup (8 ounces) reduced-fat sour cream

In a large skillet, cook beef and garlic over medium heat until meat is no longer pink; drain. Add the tomato sauce, water, tomato paste, bay leaves, parsley and Italian seasoning. Bring to a boil; reduce heat. Simmer, uncovered, for 30-40 minutes.

Discard bay leaves. Spread 1/2 cup meat sauce in a 13-in. x 9-in. baking dish coated with cooking spray. Arrange five noodles over sauce, cutting to fit. Spread with cottage cheese. Cover with five noodles, half of the meat sauce and the zucchini. Cover with five noodles and sour cream. Top with remaining noodles and meat sauce.

Bake, uncovered, at 350° for 30-35 minutes or until heated through. Let stand for 15 minutes before cutting. **YIELD: 12 SERVINGS.**

NUTRITION FACTS: 1 piece equals 187 calories, 8 g fat (0 saturated fat), 21 mg cholesterol, 270 mg sodium, 19 g carbohydrate, 2 g fiber, 14 g protein. **DIABETIC EXCHANGES:** 1 starch, 1 lean meat, 1 vegetable, 1/2 fat.

pepper-topped beef sandwiches

Bright colorful red and green peppers not only provide a mouthwatering way to perk up plain roast beef sandwiches, they're also chock-full of phytochemicals, the natural chemicals in vegetables that bolster immunity and fight disease.
—Leota Recknor, Ash Grove, Missouri

1	medium onion, chopped
2	garlic cloves, minced
1	tablespoon olive oil
1	medium sweet red pepper, julienned
1	medium green pepper, julienned
1	bay leaf

pepper-topped beef sandwiches

1/2	teaspoon salt
1/8	teaspoon pepper
1	tablespoon sugar
12	ounces thinly sliced deli roast beef
6	sandwich rolls, split

In a nonstick skillet, saute onion and garlic in oil until tender. Add the red and green peppers, bay leaf, salt and pepper. Cook and stir until peppers are tender, about 10 minutes. Add sugar; cover and simmer for 10-15 minutes or until heated through.

Discard bay leaf. Place beef on rolls; top with pepper mixture. **YIELD: 6 SERVINGS.**

NUTRITION FACTS: 1 sandwich equals 325 calories, 8 g fat (2 g saturated fat), 39 mg cholesterol, 546 mg sodium, 39 g carbohydrate, 3 g fiber, 23 g protein. **DIABETIC EXCHANGES:** 2 starch, 2 lean meat, 1 vegetable, 1/2 fat.

cilantro lime cod ⓛⓒ ⓛⓢ

My daughter loves to cook and especially likes dishes with Mexican flair. She bakes these wonderfully flavored fish fillets in foil to keep them moist and cut down on cleanup.
—Donna Hackman, Bedford, Virginia

4	cod *or* flounder fillets (2 pounds)
1/4	teaspoon pepper
1	tablespoon dried minced onion
1	garlic clove, minced
1	tablespoon olive oil
1-1/2	teaspoons ground cumin
1/4	cup minced fresh cilantro
2	limes, thinly sliced
2	tablespoons reduced-fat margarine, melted

Place each fillet on a 15-in. x 12-in. piece of heavy-duty foil. Sprinkle with pepper. In a small saucepan, saute onion and garlic in oil; stir in cumin. Spoon over fillets; sprinkle with cilantro. Place lime slices over each; drizzle with margarine. Fold foil around fish and seal tightly.

Place on a baking sheet. Bake at 375° for 35-40 minutes or until fish flakes easily with a fork. **YIELD: 8 SERVINGS.**

NUTRITION FACTS: 4 ounces cod equals 96 calories, 4 g fat (0 saturated fat), 30 mg cholesterol, 77 mg sodium, 3 g carbohydrate, 0 fiber, 13 g protein. **DIABETIC EXCHANGES:** 2 very lean meat, 1/2 fat.

roasted veggie wraps ⓂⓁ

Give roasted veggies an Italian accent with salad dressing mix and shredded mozzarella, then fold them into flour tortillas. My husband and I really enjoy the assortment of vegetables in these handheld sandwiches. They make a great light lunch.
—Jeanette Simec, Ottawa, Illinois

1 envelope Parmesan Italian salad dressing mix
1/4 cup water
1/4 cup red wine vinegar
2 tablespoons olive oil
1 medium sweet red pepper, sliced
1 cup julienned carrots
1 cup quartered fresh mushrooms
1 cup fresh broccoli florets
1 medium onion, sliced and separated into rings
1 medium yellow summer squash, sliced
6 flour tortillas (8 inches)
1-1/2 cups (6 ounces) shredded part-skim mozzarella cheese
Salsa, optional

In a jar with a tight-fitting lid, combine the dressing mix, water, vinegar and oil; shake well. Place vegetables in a large bowl; drizzle with dressing and toss to coat.

Spread vegetables in two 15-in. x 10-in. x 1-in. baking pans coated with cooking spray. Bake, uncovered, at 425° for 20-25 minutes or until tender, stirring occasionally.

Spoon about 3/4 cup roasted vegetables off center on each tortilla; sprinkle each with 1/4 cup mozzarella cheese. Place on a baking sheet.

Broil 4-6 in. from the heat for 2 minutes or until cheese is melted. Fold sides and one end of tortilla over filling and roll up. Serve with salsa if desired. **YIELD: 6 SERVINGS.**

NUTRITION FACTS: 1 wrap equals 299 calories, 12 g fat (4 g saturated fat), 16 mg cholesterol, 849 mg sodium, 35 g carbohydrate, 2 g fiber, 13 g protein. **DIABETIC EXCHANGES:** 2 vegetable, 1-1/2 starch, 1-1/2 fat, 1 lean meat.

chicken 'n' biscuits

This comforting casserole has a interesting medley of vegetables and chunky chicken topped with golden homemade biscuits.
—Marilyn Minnick, Hillsboro, Indiana

1 medium onion, chopped
2 teaspoons canola oil
1/4 cup all-purpose flour
1/2 teaspoon dried basil
1/2 teaspoon dried thyme
1/4 teaspoon pepper
2-1/2 cups fat-free milk
1 tablespoon Worcestershire sauce
1 package (16 ounces) frozen mixed vegetables
2 cups cubed cooked chicken
2 tablespoons grated Parmesan cheese
BISCUITS:
1 cup all-purpose flour
1 tablespoon sugar
1-1/2 teaspoons baking powder
1/4 teaspoon salt
1/3 cup fat-free milk
3 tablespoons canola oil
1 tablespoon minced fresh parsley

In a large saucepan, saute onion in oil until tender. Stir in the flour, basil, thyme and pepper until blended. Gradually stir in milk and Worcestershire sauce until smooth. Bring to a boil; cook and stir for 2 minutes or until thickened. Stir in the vegetables, chicken and Parmesan cheese; reduce heat to low.

Meanwhile, in a large bowl, combine the flour, sugar, baking powder and salt. In a small bowl, combine the milk, oil and parsley; stir into the dry ingredients just until combined.

Transfer hot chicken mixture to a greased 2-1/2-qt. baking dish. Drop biscuit batter by rounded tablespoonfuls onto chicken mixture.

Bake, uncovered, at 375° for 30-40 minutes or until biscuits are lightly browned. **YIELD: 8 SERVINGS.**

NUTRITION FACTS: 1 serving equals 246 calories, 8 g fat (0 saturated fat), 24 mg cholesterol, 284 mg sodium, 31 g carbohydrate, 0 fiber, 13 g protein. **DIABETIC EXCHANGES:** 2 starch, 1 meat, 1/2 fat.

chicken 'n' biscuits

roasted veggie sandwiches ⓂⓁ

Looking for a delicious way to use a variety of veggies? Try tucking your garden harvest into this hearty sandwich. The pleasant flavor of eggplant, red pepper, onion, zucchini and yellow summer squash is enhanced by a creamy basil yogurt spread. The bright blend of colors is sure to perk appetites, too!
—Taste of Home Test Kitchen

3	tablespoons balsamic vinegar
2	teaspoons olive oil
1/4	cup minced fresh basil *or* 1 tablespoon dried basil
1	small eggplant, peeled and sliced lengthwise
1	medium sweet red pepper, sliced
1	small red onion, sliced and separated into rings
1	small zucchini, thinly sliced
1	small yellow summer squash, thinly sliced

BASIL YOGURT SPREAD:

1/4	cup fat-free plain yogurt
2	tablespoons reduced-fat mayonnaise
1	tablespoon minced fresh basil *or* 1 teaspoon dried basil
1	teaspoon lemon juice
4	French rolls, split and warmed

In a large bowl, combine the vinegar, oil and basil. Add the eggplant, red pepper, onion, zucchini and yellow squash; toss to coat. Place vegetables in a single layer in a large roasting pan. Roast, uncovered, at 450° for 20-30 minutes or until tender, stirring occasionally.

Meanwhile, in a small bowl, combine the yogurt, mayonnaise, basil and lemon juice. Hollow out rolls if necessary. Serve roasted vegetables on rolls with yogurt spread. **YIELD: 4 SERVINGS.**

NUTRITION FACTS: 1 sandwich equals 275 calories, 7 g fat (1 g saturated fat), 3 mg cholesterol, 421 mg sodium, 47 g carbohydrate, 8 g fiber, 9 g protein. **DIABETIC EXCHANGES:** 3 vegetable, 2 starch, 1 fat.

roasted veggie sandwiches

apricot-stuffed turkey breast

apricot-stuffed turkey breast

For a new take on turkey, give this recipe a try. It cooks on the grill, and it's stuffed with a sensational apricot mixture.
—Bonnie De Meyer, New Carlisle, Indiana

1	boneless skinless turkey breast half (2-1/2 pounds)
1-1/2	cups soft bread crumbs
1/2	cup finely chopped dried apricots
1/4	cup chopped pecans, toasted
3	tablespoons water *or* unsweetened apple juice, *divided*
1	tablespoon canola oil
1/4	teaspoon garlic salt
1/4	teaspoon dried rosemary, crushed
1	tablespoon Dijon mustard

Cut a horizontal slit into thickest part of turkey to form a 5-in. x 4-in. pocket; set aside.

In a small bowl, combine the bread crumbs, apricots, pecans, 2 tablespoons water, oil, garlic salt and rosemary. Stuff into pocket of turkey. Secure opening with metal or soaked wooden skewers.

Prepare grill for indirect heat. Grill turkey, covered, over medium indirect heat for 50 minutes.

Combine mustard and remaining water; brush over turkey. Grill 10-25 minutes longer or until a meat thermometer reads 170°. Let stand for 10 minutes before slicing. **YIELD: 8 SERVINGS.**

NUTRITION FACTS: 1 serving equals 268 calories, 6 g fat, 81 mg cholesterol, 313 mg sodium, 20 g carbohydrate, 2 g fiber, 33 g protein. **DIABETIC EXCHANGES:** 4 very lean meat, 1 starch, 1/2 fruit, 1/2 fat.

Light
COOKING TIP

This Italian-inspired vegetable mix, as well as many other recipes in this book, is an excellent source of vitamin C, folate and beta-carotene, three key nutrients for fighting cancer and heart disease.

fettuccine primavera

A mild lemon sauce, seasoned with thyme lightly coats this attractive medley of tender chicken, pasta, asparagus, red pepper and peas.
—Marietta Howell, Okmulgee, Oklahoma

8	ounces uncooked fettuccine
1	cup julienned sweet red pepper
1	tablespoon canola oil
1/2	pound boneless skinless chicken breasts, cut into 1/4-inch strips
6	green onions, sliced
1/2	pound fresh asparagus, trimmed and cut into 1-inch pieces
3/4	cup chicken broth
1-1/2	teaspoons lemon juice
1/2	teaspoon salt
1/2	teaspoon dried thyme
1/2	teaspoon grated lemon peel
2/3	cup frozen peas, thawed
2	teaspoons cornstarch
1	tablespoon water
2	tablespoons reduced-fat sour cream
1/4	cup shredded Parmesan cheese

Cook fettuccine according to package directions. Meanwhile, in a 12-in. nonstick skillet, saute red pepper in oil for 3 minutes or until crisp-tender. Stir in the chicken, onions, asparagus, broth, lemon juice, salt, thyme and lemon peel. Cook for 1 minute or until the asparagus is crisp-tender.

Stir in peas; saute for 1 minute or until heated through. Combine cornstarch and water until smooth; stir into chicken mixture. Bring to a boil; cook and stir for 1-2 minutes or until thickened and chicken is no longer pink.

Remove from the heat; stir in sour cream. Transfer to a large bowl. Drain the fettuccine and add to chicken mixture. Sprinkle with Parmesan cheese and toss to coat. **YIELD: 6 SERVINGS.**

NUTRITION FACTS: 1-1/3 cups equals 274 calories, 6 g fat (2 g saturated fat), 27 mg cholesterol, 431 mg sodium, 38 g carbohydrate, 4 g fiber, 18 g protein. **DIABETIC EXCHANGES:** 2 starch, 1 very lean meat, 1 vegetable, 1 fat.

italian turkey cutlets ⓛⓒ

I'm watching my weight, so I make this dish often. Served with a tasteful tomato sauce, these cutlets taste so good that my son, who is thin and doesn't need to worry about his weight, requests them for his birthday dinner!
—Janet Bumb, Beallsville, Maryland

1	small onion, finely chopped
2	garlic cloves, minced
5	teaspoons olive oil, *divided*
1	can (14-1/2 ounces) Italian stewed tomatoes
1	teaspoon dried basil
1	teaspoon dried oregano
1/2	teaspoon dried rosemary, crushed
1-1/4	pounds turkey breast cutlets
1/2	teaspoon salt
1/8	teaspoon pepper
2	tablespoons shredded Parmesan cheese

In a large saucepan, saute onion and garlic in 2 teaspoons oil until tender. Stir in the tomatoes, basil, oregano and rosemary. Bring to a boil. Reduce heat; cook, uncovered, over medium heat for 15-20 minutes or until the sauce thickens.

Meanwhile, sprinkle both sides of turkey cutlets with salt and pepper. In a large nonstick over medium heat, cook turkey in batches in remaining oil until juices run clear. Serve with tomato sauce. Sprinkle with Parmesan cheese. **YIELD: 4 SERVINGS.**

NUTRITION FACTS: 1 serving equals 263 calories, 7 g fat (2 g saturated fat), 90 mg cholesterol, 750 mg sodium, 11 g carbohydrate, 3 g fiber, 37 g protein. **DIABETIC EXCHANGES:** 5 very lean meat, 2 vegetable, 1/2 fat.

fettuccine primavera

fresh marinara sauce

fresh marinara sauce ⓂⓁ

My family loves this zesty meatless sauce served over penne pasta. When tomatoes and carrots are ripe and plentiful, I double the recipe and store it in the freezer for future use.
—Martha Robinson, Homer, Michigan

3	large carrots, finely chopped
2	large onions, chopped
6	garlic cloves, minced
1/3	cup olive oil
15	medium tomatoes (about 6 pounds), peeled and chopped
1/3	cup chopped fresh basil *or* 2 tablespoons dried basil
3	tablespoons chopped fresh oregano *or* 1 tablespoon dried oregano
1-1/2	teaspoons salt
1/4	teaspoon pepper
7	cups cooked penne *or* bow tie pasta

In a Dutch oven, saute the carrots, onions and garlic in oil until tender. Add tomatoes and seasonings; bring to a boil. Reduce heat; simmer, uncovered, for 1 to 1-1/2 hours or until thickened and reduced by half, stirring occasionally. Serve with pasta. **YIELD: 7 SERVINGS.**

NUTRITION FACTS: 1 cup sauce with 1 cup pasta equals 400 calories, 12 g fat (2 g saturated fat), 0 cholesterol, 558 mg sodium, 65 g carbohydrate, 7 g fiber, 11 g protein. **DIABETIC EXCHANGES:** 3 starch, 2-1/2 vegetable, 2 fat.

vegetable chicken stir-fry ⓁⒸ

Delight your taste buds with this tangy mix of brightly colored vegetables and lean chicken breast.
—Michelle Haviland, Healdsburg, California

1	tablespoon cornstarch
1	cup reduced-sodium chicken broth
1/4	cup reduced-sodium soy sauce
1	pound boneless skinless chicken breasts, cut into strips
3	garlic cloves, minced
Dash ground ginger	
2	tablespoons olive oil, *divided*
2	cups fresh broccoli florets
1	cup fresh cauliflowerets
1	cup sliced fresh carrots
1	cup fresh *or* frozen snow peas
1	teaspoon sesame seeds, toasted

In a small bowl, combine the cornstarch, broth and soy sauce until smooth; set aside. In a large nonstick skillet, stir-fry the chicken, garlic and ginger in hot oil for 4-5 minutes or until the chicken is no longer pink. Remove and keep warm.

In a large skillet, stir-fry broccoli, cauliflower and carrots in the remaining oil for 4 minutes or until crisp-tender. Add snow peas; stir-fry for 2 minutes. Stir broth mixture; add to pan. Bring to a boil; cook and stir for 1 minute or until thickened. Add chicken; cook until heated through. Top with sesame seeds. **YIELD: 4 SERVINGS.**

NUTRITION FACTS: 1-1/2 cups equals 256 calories, 9 g fat (1 g saturated fat), 66 mg cholesterol, 862 mg sodium, 13 g carbohydrate, 2 g fiber, 31 g protein. **DIABETIC EXCHANGES:** 3 lean meat, 2 vegetable, 1 fat.

vegetable chicken stir-fry

summertime chicken tacos

summertime chicken tacos

Try these tempting tacos when you're looking for a change of pace from regular tacos.
—*Susan Scott, Asheville, North Carolina*

1/3	cup olive oil
1/4	cup lime juice
4	garlic cloves, minced
1	tablespoon minced fresh parsley *or* 1 teaspoon dried parsley flakes
1	teaspoon ground cumin
1	teaspoon dried oregano
1/2	teaspoon salt, optional
1/4	teaspoon pepper
4	boneless skinless chicken breast halves (1-1/4 pounds)
6	flour tortillas (8 inches) *or* taco shells, warmed

Toppings of your choice

In a large resealable plastic bag, combine the first eight ingredients; add chicken. Seal bag and turn to coat. Refrigerate for 8 hours or overnight, turning occasionally.

Drain and discard marinade. Grill chicken, uncovered, over medium heat for 5-7 minutes on each side or until a meat thermometer reads 170°. Cut chicken into thin strips; serve in tortilla or taco shells with desired toppings. **YIELD: 6 SERVINGS.**

NUTRITION FACTS: 1 flour chicken tortilla (calculated without salt and toppings) equals 338 calories, 12 g fat (0 saturated fat), 63 mg cholesterol, 289 mg sodium, 28 g carbohydrate, 0 fiber, 27 g protein. **DIABETIC EXCHANGES:** 3 lean meat, 2 starch, 1/2 fat.

asparagus ham dinner

I've been making this light meal for my family for years, and it's always well received. With asparagus, tomato, pasta and chunks of ham, it's a tempting blend of tastes and textures.
—*Rhonda Zavodny, David City, Nebraska*

2	cups uncooked spiral pasta
3/4	pound fresh asparagus, cut into 1-inch pieces
1	medium sweet yellow pepper, julienned
1	tablespoon olive oil
3	cups diced fresh tomatoes (about 6 medium)
6	ounces reduced-sodium fully cooked ham, cubed
1/4	cup minced fresh parsley
1/2	teaspoon salt
1/2	teaspoon dried oregano
1/2	teaspoon dried basil
1/8	to 1/4 teaspoon cayenne pepper
1/4	cup shredded Parmesan cheese

Cook pasta according to package directions. Meanwhile, in a nonstick skillet, saute asparagus and yellow pepper in oil until tender. Add tomatoes and ham; heat through.

Drain pasta; add to the vegetable mixture. Stir in seasonings. Sprinkle with cheese. **YIELD: 6 SERVINGS.**

NUTRITION FACTS: 1-1/3 cups equals 238 calories, 6 g fat (1 g saturated fat), 18 mg cholesterol, 522 mg sodium, 33 g carbohydrate, 3 g fiber, 14 g protein. **DIABETIC EXCHANGES:** 2 vegetable, 1-1/2 starch, 1 lean meat, 1/2 fat.

asparagus ham dinner

zucchini crust pizza LC ML

My mother-in-law gave me the recipe for this unique pizza. Its quiche-like zucchini crust packs a lot of protein and makes it just right for brunch, lunch or a light supper.
—Ruth Denomme, Englehart, Ontario

- 3 cups shredded zucchini
- 3/4 cup egg substitute
- 1/3 cup all-purpose flour
- 1/2 teaspoon salt
- 2 cups (8 ounces) shredded part-skim mozzarella cheese
- 2 small tomatoes, halved and thinly sliced
- 1/2 cup chopped onion
- 1/2 cup julienned green pepper
- 1 teaspoon dried oregano
- 1/2 teaspoon dried basil
- 3 tablespoons shredded Parmesan cheese

In a large bowl, combine zucchini and egg substitute. Stir in flour and salt. Spread onto the bottom of a 12-in. pizza pan coated with cooking spray.

Bake at 450° for 8 minutes. Reduce heat to 350°. Sprinkle with the mozzarella cheese, tomatoes, onion, green pepper, oregano, basil and Parmesan cheese. Bake for 15-20 minutes or until onion is tender and cheese is melted. **YIELD: 6 SLICES.**

NUTRITION FACTS: 1 slice equals 190 calories, 8 g fat (5 g saturated fat), 24 mg cholesterol, 431 mg sodium, 13 g carbohydrate, 2 g fiber, 17 g protein. **DIABETIC EXCHANGES:** 2 lean meat, 2 vegetable, 1/2 fat.

broiled orange roughy

broiled orange roughy LC

This entree is guaranteed to catch anyone's fancy. The fillets are flaky, juicy and mildly flavored. They can be broiled in the oven, but I often cook them on our outdoor grill to reduce kitchen cleanup.
—Judy Bernacki, Las Vegas, Nevada

- 1/4 cup butter, melted
- 1/4 cup lemon juice
- 1/4 cup soy sauce
- 1 teaspoon garlic powder
- 1-1/2 pounds orange roughy, red snapper *or* haddock fillets

Paprika

In a large resealable plastic bag, combine the butter, lemon juice, soy sauce and garlic powder; add fish. Seal bag and turn to coat. Marinate for 10 minutes.

Drain and discard marinade. Place fish on a broiler pan. Broil 3-4 in. from the heat for 5 minutes on each side or until fish flakes easily with a fork. Sprinkle with paprika. **YIELD: 4 SERVINGS.**

NUTRITION FACTS: 1 orange roughy fillet (prepared with reduced-sodium soy sauce) equals 189 calories, 7 g fat (4 g saturated fat), 50 mg cholesterol, 489 mg sodium, 5 g carbohydrate, trace fiber, 26 g protein. **DIABETIC EXCHANGES:** 4 very lean meat, 1 fat.

zucchini crust pizza

Light COOKING TIP

Lemon and lime juice or zest can be used interchangeably in equal amounts in most recipes. Add a little of both to this fish entree for a refreshing lemon/lime flavor.

tomato meat loaf

Topped with slices of tomato, this tender beef loaf looks fancy but is actually easy to fix. It's delicious served alongside a fresh green salad or a small baked potato.

—Linda Begley, Stoutsville, Missouri

1	egg, lightly beaten
1/2	cup fat-free milk
1/4	cup ketchup
1	cup quick-cooking oats
1	slice white bread, crumbled
4	saltines, crushed
1/2	teaspoon salt
1/4	teaspoon pepper
2	pounds lean ground beef
1	medium tomato, sliced

In a large bowl, combine the first eight ingredients. Crumble beef over mixture and mix well. Shape into a loaf in a greased 13-in. x 9-in. baking dish. Bake, uncovered, at 350° for 1 hour.

Arrange tomato slices over loaf. Bake 30 minutes longer or until meat is no longer pink and a meat thermometer reads 160°. Using two large spatulas, carefully transfer meat loaf to a serving platter. YIELD: 8 SERVINGS.

NUTRITION FACTS: 1 serving equals 299 calories, 13 g fat (5 g saturated fat), 69 mg cholesterol, 442 mg sodium, 17 g carbohydrate, 1 g fiber, 27 g protein. **DIABETIC EXCHANGES:** 3 lean meat, 1 starch, 1 fat.

chicken and herbs Ⓛⓒ

This moist and tender chicken is nicely seasoned with a variety of herbs, and hot pepper sauce gives it a little extra kick. It's easy to prepare and good for you, too.

—Judy Sargent, Rome, New York

4	bone-in chicken breast halves (2 pounds)
2	tablespoons olive oil
1	tablespoon grated onion
2	garlic cloves, minced
1	teaspoon dried thyme
1/2	teaspoon salt
1/2	teaspoon dried rosemary, crushed
1/2	teaspoon coarsely ground pepper
1/4	teaspoon rubbed sage
1/8	teaspoon dried marjoram
1/8	teaspoon hot pepper sauce
4-1/2	teaspoons minced fresh parsley

Arrange chicken in an 11-in. x 7-in. baking dish coated with cooking spray. Whisk together the oil, onion, garlic, thyme, salt, rosemary, pepper, sage, marjoram and hot pepper sauce. Pour over chicken.

Bake, uncovered, at 425° for 30-40 minutes or until a meat thermometer reads 170°, basting occasionally. Remove and discard skin from chicken. Sprinkle with parsley. Drizzle with juice. YIELD: 4 SERVINGS.

NUTRITION FACTS: 1 chicken breast half with 1 tablespoon juice equals 240 calories, 11 g fat (2 g saturated fat), 90 mg cholesterol, 373 mg sodium, 1 g carbohydrate, trace fiber, 33 g protein. **DIABETIC EXCHANGES:** 4 lean meat, 1 fat.

baked chicken fajitas

I can't remember when or where I found this recipe, but I've prepared it almost every week since. We like it with hot sauce for a little added zip.

—Amy Trinkle, Milwaukee, Wisconsin

1	pound boneless skinless chicken breasts, cut into thin strips
1	can (14-1/2 ounces) diced tomatoes and green chilies, drained
1	medium onion, cut into thin strips
1	medium green pepper, cut into thin strips
1	medium sweet red pepper, cut into thin strips
2	tablespoons canola oil
2	teaspoons chili powder
2	teaspoons ground cumin
1/4	teaspoon salt
12	flour tortillas (6 inches), warmed

In a 13-in. x 9-in. baking dish coated with cooking spray, combine the chicken, tomatoes, onion and peppers. Combine the oil, chili powder, cumin and salt. Drizzle over chicken mixture; toss to coat.

Bake, uncovered, at 400° for 20-25 minutes or until chicken is no longer pink and vegetables are tender. Spoon onto tortillas; fold in sides. YIELD: 6 SERVINGS.

NUTRITION FACTS: Two fajitas equals 340 calories, 8 g fat (1 g saturated fat), 44 mg cholesterol, 330 mg sodium, 41 g carbohydrate, 5 g fiber, 27 g protein. **DIABETIC EXCHANGES:** 2 starch, 2 lean meat, 2 vegetable, 1/2 fat.

baked chicken fajitas

desserts & beverages

chocolate cupcakes
page 100

light lemon cheesecake

light lemon cheesecake (ML)

My family loves cheesecake, but we don't care for the fat that usually comes with it. This pretty fruit-topped alternative offers a creamy texture and full flavor without the guilt!

—*Deborah Lobe, Olympia, Washington*

3/4	cup reduced-fat cinnamon graham cracker crumbs (about 4 whole crackers)
3	packages (8 ounces *each*) fat-free cream cheese
2	packages (8 ounces *each*) reduced-fat cream cheese
1-2/3	cups sugar
1/8	teaspoon salt
9	egg whites
1/4	cup lemon juice
1-1/2	teaspoons vanilla extract
1	teaspoon grated lemon peel
8	strawberries, sliced
2	medium kiwifruit, peeled and sliced

Sprinkle graham cracker crumbs on the bottom and up the sides of a 9-in. springform pan well coated with cooking spray; set aside.

In a large bowl, beat the cream cheese, sugar and salt until smooth. Add egg whites; beat on low speed just until combined. Stir in the lemon juice, vanilla and lemon peel.

Pour into prepared pan. Bake at 325° for 70-80 minutes or until the center is almost set. Cool on a wire rack for 10 minutes. Carefully run a knife around edge of pan to loosen; cool 1 hour longer. Refrigerate overnight. Top with strawberries and kiwi. **YIELD: 12 SERVINGS.**

NUTRITION FACTS: 1 slice equals 300 calories, 8 g fat (5 g saturated fat), 26 mg cholesterol, 522 mg sodium, 42 g carbohydrate, 1 g fiber, 15 g protein. **DIABETIC EXCHANGES:** 2 fat-free milk, 1 fruit, 1 fat.

Light COOKING TIP

Even when made with lighter ingredients, cheesecakes are a luscious dessert that feed a crowd. Best of all, they can be made in advance, so there's one less thing to do on the day you're entertaining. Cheesecakes can be covered and refrigerated for up to three days.

tropical pineapple smoothies

tropical pineapple smoothies ⓛⓕ ⓛⓢ ⓜⓛ

Around our house, we often make these yummy shakes. To make the shakes healthier, we substitute fat-free milk and ice cubes for the ice cream. They are fast and nutritious!
—Polly Coumos, Mogadore, Ohio

    1   cup fat-free milk
    1   can (8 ounces) unsweetened crushed pineapple
  1/2   cup unsweetened pineapple juice
    3   tablespoons sugar
  1/2   teaspoon vanilla extract
  1/4   teaspoon coconut extract
    6   ice cubes

In a blender, place the first six ingredients; cover and process until smooth. Add ice cubes; cover and process until smooth. Pour into chilled glasses; serve immediately. **YIELD: 3 SERVINGS.**

NUTRITION FACTS: 1 cup equals 126 calories, trace fat (trace saturated fat), 2 mg cholesterol, 45 mg sodium, 29 g carbohydrate, 1 g fiber, 3 g protein. **DIABETIC EXCHANGES:** 1 fruit, 1/2 starch, 1/2 fat-free milk.

banana cupcakes ⓜⓛ

These cupcakes are high in potassium, making them a great snack anytime of day or even for a post-workout treat.
—Arloia Lutz, Sebewaing, Michigan

  1/3   cup shortening
  2/3   cup sugar
    1   egg
    1   teaspoon vanilla extract
  3/4   cup mashed ripe bananas (about 2 small bananas)
1-1/3   cups cake flour
    1   teaspoon baking powder
  1/2   teaspoon salt
  1/2   teaspoon baking soda
  1/2   teaspoon ground cinnamon
  1/2   teaspoon ground cloves
  1/4   teaspoon ground nutmeg
    1   tablespoon confectioners' sugar

In a large bowl, cream shortening and sugar until light and fluffy. Beat in the egg, vanilla and bananas. Combine the flour, baking powder, salt, baking soda, cinnamon, cloves and nutmeg; add to the creamed mixture just until combined.

Fill paper-lined muffin cups two-thirds full. Bake at 375° for 18-20 minutes or until a toothpick comes out clean. Cool for 10 minutes before removing from pan to a wire rack to cool completely. Dust with confectioners' sugar. **YIELD: 1 DOZEN.**

NUTRITION FACTS: 1 cupcake equals 154 calories, 6 g fat (2 g saturated fat), 18 mg cholesterol, 175 mg sodium, 24 g carbohydrate, 1 g fiber, 2 g protein. **DIABETIC EXCHANGES:** 1-1/2 starch, 1 fat.

cream-topped grapes ⓛⓕ ⓛⓢ ⓜⓛ

I dress up bunches of red and green grapes with a decadent dressing that comes together in no time. You can also dollop the heavenly four-ingredient sauce over your favorite combination of fruit.
—Vioda Geyer, Uhrichsville, Ohio

    4   ounces reduced-fat cream cheese, softened
  1/4   cup sugar
  1/2   teaspoon vanilla extract
  1/2   cup reduced-fat sour cream
    3   cups seedless green grapes
    3   cups seedless red grapes

In a small bowl, beat the cream cheese, sugar and vanilla. Add the sour cream; mix well. Divide grapes among individual serving bowls; dollop with topping. **YIELD: 8 SERVINGS.**

NUTRITION FACTS: 3/4 cup grapes plus 2 tablespoons topping (prepared with reduced-fat cream cheese and fat-free sour cream) equals 120 calories, 3 g fat (2 g saturated fat), 8 mg cholesterol, 55 mg sodium, 22 g carbohydrate, 1 g fiber, 3 g protein. **DIABETIC EXCHANGES:** 1-1/2 fruit, 1/2 fat.

makeover streusel coffee cake

makeover streusel coffee cake (ML)

Our home economists slimmed down this coffee cake recipe without losing any flavor. The result was a coffee cake with almost 30% fewer calories, 40% less fat and about 55% less saturated fat and cholesterol.

—*Taste of Home Test Kitchen*

- 2/3 cup chopped walnuts
- 1/3 cup packed brown sugar
- 1 tablespoon butter, melted
- 1/2 teaspoon ground cinnamon

COFFEE CAKE:

- 1/4 cup butter, softened
- 1-1/4 cups sugar
- 2 egg yolks
- 1/4 cup canola oil
- 1/4 cup unsweetened applesauce
- 1 teaspoon vanilla extract
- 3 cups cake flour
- 2 teaspoons baking powder
- 1 teaspoon baking soda
- 1/4 teaspoon salt
- 1-1/2 cups reduced-fat sour cream
- 4 egg whites
- 2 teaspoons confectioners' sugar

In a small bowl, combine the nuts, brown sugar, butter and cinnamon; set aside. In a large bowl, cream butter and sugar until light and crumbly. Beat in the egg yolks, oil, applesauce and vanilla. Combine the dry ingredients; add to the sugar mixture alternately with sour cream, beating well after each addition.

In another bowl, beat egg whites on high speed until stiff peaks form. Fold into batter.

Pour half of the batter into a 10-in. fluted tube pan coated with cooking spray and floured; sprinkle with nut mixture. Pour in remaining batter.

Bake at 350° for 45-55 minutes or until a toothpick inserted near the center comes out clean. Cool for 10 minutes before removing from pan to a wire rack to cool completely. Sprinkle with confectioners' sugar. **YIELD: 14 SERVINGS.**

NUTRITION FACTS: 1 slice equals 328 calories, 14 g fat (5 g saturated fat), 50 mg cholesterol, 288 mg sodium, 48 g carbohydrate, 1 g fiber, 5 g protein. **DIABETIC EXCHANGES:** 3 starch, 2 fat.

fruity summer cooler (LS) (ML)

When the melons first come in, we make this delightful, thirst-quenching cooler. Cantaloupe and pineapple are a great flavor combination.

—*Ruth Andrewson, Leavenworth, Washington*

- 6 to 8 ice cubes
- 1/2 cup cubed cantaloupe
- 1/2 cup pineapple chunks
- 1/2 cup cranberry juice
- 1/3 cup sliced banana
- 1/4 cup pineapple juice
- 1 tablespoon honey
- 3/4 teaspoon lemon juice
- 1/4 teaspoon grated lemon peel

In a blender, combine all the ingredients; cover and process until smooth. Pour into chilled glasses; serve immediately. **YIELD: 2-3 SERVINGS.**

NUTRITION FACTS: 1 cup equals 102 calories, trace fat (trace saturated fat), 0 cholesterol, 4 mg sodium, 27 g carbohydrate, 1 g fiber, 1 g protein. **DIABETIC EXCHANGE:** 1-1/2 fruit.

fruity summer cooler

double chocolate cupcakes

double chocolate cupcakes (LF) (ML)

You don't have to fudge on chocolate to make a light and luscious treat. These moist cupcakes are chock-full of sweet flavor, but low in saturated fat.

—Linda Utter, Sidney, Montana

2	tablespoons butter, softened
3/4	cup sugar
1	egg
1	egg white
1/2	cup plus 2 tablespoons buttermilk
1/3	cup water
1	tablespoon white vinegar
1	teaspoon vanilla extract
1-1/2	cups all-purpose flour
1/4	cup baking cocoa
1	teaspoon baking soda
1/2	teaspoon salt
1/3	cup miniature semisweet chocolate chips

In a large bowl, cream butter and sugar until light and fluffy. Add egg and egg white, one at a time, beating well after each addition. Beat on high speed until light and fluffy. Stir in the buttermilk, water, vinegar and vanilla. Combine the flour, cocoa, baking soda and salt; add to batter just until moistened. Stir in chocolate chips.

Fill muffin cups coated with cooking spray three-fourths full. Bake at 375° for 15-18 minutes or until a toothpick comes out clean. Cool for 5 minutes before removing from pans to wire racks. **YIELD: 14 CUPCAKES.**

NUTRITION FACTS: 1 cupcake equals 139 calories, 2 g fat (1 g saturated fat), 1 mg cholesterol, 221 mg sodium, 29 g carbohydrate, 1 g fiber, 3 g protein. **DIABETIC EXCHANGES:** 1-1/2 starch, 1/2 fat.

peach smoothies (LS) (ML)

Whip up this refreshing drink for a nutritious snack or a quick chilled breakfast. The recipe calls for frozen fruit, so you don't have to wait until summer when peaches are in season to enjoy this delicious drink.

—Dana Tittle, Forest City, Alaska

2	cups milk
2	cups frozen unsweetened sliced peaches
1/4	cup orange juice concentrate
2	tablespoons sugar
5	ice cubes

In a blender, combine all ingredients; cover and process until smooth. Pour into chilled glasses; serve immediately. **YIELD: 4 SERVINGS.**

NUTRITION FACTS: 1 cup equals 143 calories, 4 g fat (3 g saturated fat), 17 mg cholesterol, 60 mg sodium, 23 g carbohydrate, 2 g fiber, 5 g protein. **DIABETIC EXCHANGES:** 1/2 milk, 1 fruit.

peach smoothies

luscious lime angel squares

chewy oatmeal raisin cookies ⓁⓈ ⓂⓁ

Even picky eaters devour these wholesome treats sprinkled with cinnamon and packed with raisins. Washed down with a glass of milk, the cookies are also great as an on-the-go breakfast.
—*Trina Boitnott, Boones Mill, Virginia*

1/3	cup canola oil
1/3	cup packed brown sugar
2	tablespoons sugar
3	tablespoons water
1	egg white
3/4	teaspoon vanilla extract
1/3	cup all-purpose flour
1/3	cup whole wheat flour
2	teaspoons ground cinnamon
1/2	teaspoon baking soda
1/4	teaspoon salt
2	cups old-fashioned oats
1/2	cup raisins

In a large bowl, combine the oil, sugars, water, egg white and vanilla. Combine the flours, cinnamon, baking soda and salt; gradually add to sugar mixture and mix well. Stir in oats and raisins.

Drop by scant 1/4 cupfuls onto baking sheets coated with cooking spray; flatten slightly with the back of a spoon. Bake at 350° for 10-12 minutes or until golden brown. Cool for 1 minute before removing from pans to wire racks. **YIELD: 15 COOKIES.**

NUTRITION FACTS: 1 cookie equals 144 calories, 6 g fat (1 g saturated fat), 0 cholesterol, 88 mg sodium, 22 g carbohydrate, 2 g fiber, 3 g protein. **DIABETIC EXCHANGES:** 1-1/2 starch, 1 fat.

luscious lime angel squares ⓂⓁ

A creamy lime topping turns angel food cake into these yummy squares perfect for potlucks or picnics. I altered the original recipe to use reduced-fat ingredients, so you can eat a piece of this airy dessert without feeling one bit guilty.
—*Beverly Marshall, Orting, Washington*

1	package (.3 ounces) sugar-free lime gelatin
1	cup boiling water
1	prepared angel food cake (8 inches), cut into 1-inch cubes
1	package (8 ounces) reduced-fat cream cheese, cubed
1/2	cup sugar
2	teaspoons lemon juice
1-1/2	teaspoons grated lemon peel
1	carton (8 ounces) reduced-fat whipped topping, thawed, *divided*

In a bowl, dissolve gelatin in boiling water. Refrigerate until mixture just begins to thicken, about 35 minutes. Place cake cubes in a 13-in. x 9-in. dish coated with cooking spray; set aside.

In a small bowl, beat cream cheese until smooth. Beat in the sugar, lemon juice and peel. Add gelatin mixture; beat until combined. Fold in 1-1/2 cups whipped topping.

Spread over top of cake, covering completely. Refrigerate for at least 2 hours or until firm. Cut into squares; top with remaining whipped topping. **YIELD: 15 SERVINGS.**

NUTRITION FACTS: 1 piece equals 139 calories, 4 g fat (3 g saturated fat), 8 mg cholesterol, 145 mg sodium, 21 g carbohydrate, trace fiber, 3 g protein. **DIABETIC EXCHANGES:** 1-1/2 starch, 1 fat.

chewy oatmeal raisin cookies

banana cocoa smoothies

banana cocoa smoothies ⓛⓕ ⓛⓢ ⓜⓛ

With its chocolaty twist, this frothy concoction appeals to folks of all ages. It's a great way to ensure youngsters get plenty of calcium-packed yogurt and milk, too.
—*Anne Yaeger, Houston, Texas*

1	cup (8 ounces) fat-free vanilla yogurt
3/4	cup fat-free milk
1	medium ripe banana, frozen and cut into chunks
3	tablespoons sugar-free chocolate drink mix
1/4	teaspoon vanilla extract

In a blender, combine all ingredients. Cover and process until smooth. Pour into chilled glasses; serve immediately. **YIELD: 3 SERVINGS.**

NUTRITION FACTS: 1 cup equals 155 calories, 1 g fat (trace saturated fat), 3 mg cholesterol, 100 mg sodium, 30 g carbohydrate, 2 g fiber, 7 g protein. **DIABETIC EXCHANGES:** 1 fruit, 1 fat-free milk.

chocolate eclair dessert ⓛⓒ ⓜⓛ

My father, who's diabetic, loves chocolate and baked goods. This recipe takes advantage of sugar-free and reduced-fat ingredients to create a mouth-watering confection all can enjoy.
—*Owen Jack Hiatt, Colorado Springs, Colorado*

1	cup water
1/2	cup butter, cubed
1	cup all-purpose flour
4	eggs
1	package (1.5 ounces) instant sugar-free vanilla pudding mix
2-3/4	cups fat-free milk
1	package (8 ounces) reduced-fat cream cheese, softened
1/2	cup light chocolate syrup

In a saucepan, bring water and butter to a boil, stirring constantly until butter is melted. Reduce heat to low; add the flour. Stir vigorously with a wooden spoon until mixture leaves sides of pan and forms a smooth ball. Remove from the heat.

Add eggs, one at a time, beating well after each addition until the batter becomes smooth. Spread into a greased and floured 13-in. x 9-in. baking pan. Bake at 400° for 30 minutes or until puffed and golden. Immediately remove from pan and cut in half horizontally. Cool completely.

For filling, beat pudding mix, milk and cream cheese in a bowl until smooth. Just before serving, place bottom eclair layer on a serving platter; cover with filling. Replace the top layer and drizzle with the chocolate syrup. **YIELD: 15 SERVINGS.**

NUTRITION FACTS: 1 piece equals 175 calories, 10 g fat (0 saturated fat), 65 mg cholesterol, 312 mg sodium, 15 g carbohydrate, 0 fiber, 6 g protein. **DIABETIC EXCHANGES:** 2 fat, 1 starch.

pineapple icebox dessert ⓜⓛ

While living in Italy, I fell in love with Italian tiramisu, but I didn't like all the fat and calories that came with it. So I substituted healthier ingredients to make this pineapple version.
—*Julie Vyska, North Las Vegas, Nevada*

2	cups cold fat-free milk
1	package (1 ounce) sugar-free instant vanilla pudding mix
1	cup reduced-fat whipped topping
1	can (20 ounces) pineapple tidbits
2	packages (3 ounces *each*) ladyfingers

In a large bowl, whisk milk and pudding mix for 2 minutes. Let stand for 2 minutes or until soft-set. Fold in whipped topping; set aside.

Drain pineapple, reserving 1/4 cup juice. Arrange half of the ladyfingers in an ungreased 11-in. x 7-in. dish.

Brush with 2 tablespoons reserved pineapple juice. Top with half of the pudding mixture and half of the pineapple. Repeat layers. Cover and refrigerate overnight. Cut into squares. **YIELD: 15 SERVINGS.**

NUTRITION FACTS: 1 piece equals 183 calories, 4 g fat (2 g saturated fat), 99 mg cholesterol, 234 mg sodium, 31 g carbohydrate, 1 g fiber, 5 g protein. **DIABETIC EXCHANGES:** 1 starch, 1 fruit, 1/2 fat.

raisin carrot cake

raisin carrot cake ⓂL

This is one dessert you can actually feel good about eating! Carrots add beta-carotene, soluble fiber and antioxidants.
—*Joyce Donald, Star City, Saskatchewan*

2	egg whites
3/4	cup sugar
1/2	cup unsweetened applesauce
1/4	cup canola oil
1-1/2	cups finely shredded carrots
1/2	cup reduced-fat vanilla yogurt
1/4	cup water
1	cup all-purpose flour, *divided*
1	cup whole wheat flour
2	teaspoons ground cinnamon
1-1/2	teaspoons baking soda
1/4	teaspoon salt
1/4	teaspoon ground nutmeg
1/4	teaspoon ground cloves
3/4	cup raisins
1-1/2	teaspoons confectioners' sugar

In a large bowl, beat egg whites until foamy. Beat in the sugar, applesauce and oil until well blended. Stir in the carrots, yogurt and water.

Set aside 1 tablespoon all-purpose flour. Combine the whole wheat flour, cinnamon, baking soda, salt, nutmeg, cloves and remaining all-purpose flour; add to batter just until moistened. Toss raisins with reserved flour; stir into batter.

Pour into a 9-in. square baking pan coated with cooking spray. Bake at 325° for 50-55 minutes or until a toothpick near the center comes our clean. Cool on a wire rack. Sprinkle with confectioners' sugar. **YIELD: 9 SERVINGS.**

NUTRITION FACTS: 1 piece equals 279 calories, 7 g fat (1 g saturated fat), 1 mg cholesterol, 306 mg sodium, 52 g carbohydrate, 4 g fiber, 5 g protein. **DIABETIC EXCHANGES:** 2-1/2 starch, 1 fruit, 1 fat.

honeydew kiwi cooler ⓁF ⓁS ⓂL

Our home economists suggest you make a big pitcher of this thick, fruity beverage because guests are sure to ask for a second glass! The colorful quencher has a refreshing melon flavor and gets its creamy consistency from fat-free yogurt.
—*Taste of Home Test Kitchen*

3	cups cubed honeydew
2	kiwifruit, peeled and cubed
1/2	cup fat-free plain yogurt
2	tablespoons honey
1	cup ice cubes
2	to 3 drops green food coloring, optional

In a blender, combine all ingredients; cover and process until blended. Pour into chilled glasses; serve immediately. **YIELD: 4 SERVINGS.**

NUTRITION FACTS: 1 cup equals 113 calories, trace fat (trace saturated fat), 1 mg cholesterol, 32 mg sodium, 28 g carbohydrate, 2 g fiber, 2 g protein. **DIABETIC EXCHANGE:** 2 fruit.

honeydew kiwi cooler

Light
COOKING TIP

To ripen healthful kiwifruit, place in a brown paper bag with a banana or apple and leave at room temperature. When they are ready to eat, kiwis should yield to slight pressure. Store ripe fruits in the refrigerator for up to one week.

chocolate cupcakes

chocolate cupcakes ⓂⓁ

Got a serious chocolate craving? Get your daily fix with these scrumptious cupcakes. The calorie count for one cupcake is less than a cup of flavored store-bought yogurt, but is sure to be oh-so much more satisfying. Replace the frosting with fat-free whipped topping and a sprinking of cocoa if you like.
—*Marlene Martin, Country Harbour Mines, Nova Scotia*

1/2	cup butter, softened
1	cup sugar
1	egg
1	teaspoon vanilla extract
1-1/2	cups all-purpose flour
1/2	cup baking cocoa
1	teaspoon baking soda
1/4	teaspoon salt
1/2	cup water
1/2	cup buttermilk

Frosting of your choice

In a small bowl, cream butter and sugar until light and fluffy. Beat in egg and vanilla. Combine the flour, cocoa, baking soda and salt; gradually add to creamed mixture alternately with water and buttermilk, beating well after each addition.

Fill paper-lined muffin cups two-thirds full. Bake at 375° for 12-15 minutes or until a toothpick inserted near the center comes out clean. Cool for 10 minutes before removing from pans to wire racks to cool completely. Frost cupcakes. **YIELD: 16 CUPCAKES.**

NUTRITION FACTS: 1 cupcake equals 157 calories, 6 g fat (4 g saturated fat), 29 mg cholesterol, 169 mg sodium, 23 g carbohydrate, 1 g fiber, 2 g protein. **DIABETIC EXCHANGES:** 1/2 starch, 1 fat.

lemon blueberry cheesecake ⓂⓁ

For a refreshing alternative to traditional cheesecake, try this no-bake treat. It tastes as luscious as it looks.
—*Julia Klee, Bonaire, Georgia*

1	package (3 ounces) lemon gelatin
1	cup boiling water
1	cup graham cracker crumbs
2	tablespoons butter, melted
1	tablespoon canola oil
3	cups (24 ounces) fat-free cottage cheese
1/4	cup sugar

TOPPING:

2	tablespoons sugar
1-1/2	teaspoons cornstarch
1/4	cup water
1-1/3	cups fresh *or* frozen blueberries, *divided*
1	teaspoon lemon juice

In a large bowl, dissolve gelatin in boiling water. Cool. In a small bowl, combine the crumbs, butter and oil. Press onto the bottom of a 9-in. springform pan. Chill.

In a blender, cover and process cottage cheese and sugar until smooth. While processing, slowly add cooled gelatin. Pour into crust; cover and refrigerate overnight.

For topping, in a small saucepan, combine sugar and cornstarch; gradually stir in water until smooth. Add 1 cup blueberries. Bring to a boil; cook and stir for 2 minutes or until thickened. Stir in lemon juice; cool slightly. Transfer to a blender; cover and process until smooth. Refrigerate until chilled.

Carefully run a knife around edge of pan to loosen cheesecake; remove sides of pan. Spread the blueberry mixture over the top. Sprinkle with remaining blueberries. Refrigerate leftovers. **YIELD: 12 SERVINGS.**

NUTRITION FACTS: 1 slice equals 171 calories, 4 g fat (1 g saturated fat), 8 mg cholesterol, 352 mg sodium, 27 g carbohydrate, 1 g fiber, 8 g protein. **DIABETIC EXCHANGES:** 1-1/2 starch, 1/2 fruit, 1/2 fat.

lemon blueberry cheesecake

orange angel food cake dessert

orange angel food cake dessert (LF) (ML)

Light-as-air angel food cake, sugar-free orange gelatin and sugar-free vanilla pudding help cut the fat and calories from this sunny citrus dessert that I frequently make for my family and friends. They can't seem to get enough!
—Janet Springer, St. Petersburg, Florida

1	package (16 ounces) angel food cake mix
1	package (.3 ounce) sugar-free orange gelatin
3/4	cup boiling water
1/2	cup cold water
1-1/2	cups cold fat-free milk
1	package (1 ounce) sugar-free instant vanilla pudding mix
1	teaspoon orange extract
1	carton (8 ounces) frozen reduced-fat whipped topping, thawed
1	small navel orange, halved and sliced
1/2	cup sliced almonds, toasted

Prepare and bake cake according to package directions, using an ungreased 10-in. tube pan. Immediately invert tube pan; cool completely.

In a small bowl, dissolve gelatin in boiling water; stir in cold water and set aside. Cut cake into 2-in. slices; arrange cake slices in a ungreased 13-in. x 9-in. dish. With a meat fork, poke holes about 2 in. apart into the cake. Slowly pour gelatin over cake; chill until set.

In a large bowl, whisk milk and pudding mix for 2 minutes. Whisk in extract. Let stand for 2 minutes or until soft-set. Fold in whipped topping. Spread over cake. Garnish with orange slices and almonds. Cover and refrigerate until serving. YIELD: 15 SERVINGS.

NUTRITION FACTS: 1 piece equals 184 calories, 3 g fat (2 g saturated fat), 0.55 mg cholesterol, 285 mg sodium, 32 g carbohydrate, 1 g fiber, 5 g protein. DIABETIC EXCHANGES: 2 starch, 1/2 fat.

frozen banana pops (LS) (ML)

This is a fun dessert after a casual meal or for a frosty snack. My kids love rolling the bananas in various toppings.
—Joy Cochran, Roy, Washington

1/2	cup semisweet chocolate chips
3	tablespoons honey
1/4	cup reduced-fat peanut butter
2	tablespoons fat-free milk
4	medium firm bananas, halved
8	popsicle sticks
1/3	cup finely chopped nuts

In a small heavy saucepan, melt chocolate chips and honey over low heat, stirring constantly. Add peanut butter; stir until smooth. Remove from the heat and stir in milk.

Peel bananas and insert popsicle sticks into one end. Spoon chocolate mixture over bananas to coat. Sprinkle with nuts. Place on a waxed paper-lined baking sheet. Freeze for at least 30 minutes. Serve frozen. YIELD: 8 SERVINGS.

NUTRITION FACTS: 1 pop equals 213 calories, 9 g fat (3 g saturated fat), 0.55 mg cholesterol, 67 mg sodium, 32 g carbohydrate, 3 g fiber, 5 g protein. DIABETIC EXCHANGES: 1-1/2 fat, 1 starch, 1 fruit.

peppermint ice cream cake (ML)

This fancy-looking cake is a great dessert for cleansing the palate and is sure to be a hit with guests. Replace the ice cream with fat-free frozen vanilla yogurt for a lighter version.
—Nancy Horsburgh, Everett, Ontario

1	round angel food cake (10 inches)
1	quart vanilla ice cream, slightly softened
6	chocolate-covered peppermint patties (1.5 ounces *each*), chopped
1/2	cup chopped pecans
1/8	teaspoon peppermint extract
Green food coloring, optional	

Split cake into three horizontal layers; place bottom layer on a serving plate.

In a bowl, combine ice cream, peppermint patties, pecans, extract and a few drops of food coloring if desired. Spread a third of the mixture over bottom cake layer. Top with a second cake layer and another portion of ice cream mixture; repeat layers.

Cover and freeze for up to 1 month. Remove from the freezer just before serving. YIELD: 16 SERVINGS.

NUTRITION FACTS: 1 slice (prepared with fat-free frozen vanilla yogurt) equals 224 calories, 4 g fat (0 saturated fat), 1 mg cholesterol, 228 mg sodium, 44 g carbohydrate, 0 fiber, 5 g protein. DIABETIC EXCHANGES: 2-1/2 starch, 1 fat.

lemon poppy seed cake

lemon poppy seed cake ⓂⓁ

Family and friends will love this buttermilk cake...whether you serve tender slices with coffee at brunch or as a treat after dinner. The delicate lemon glaze adds a special touch.
—*Kristen Croke, Hanover, Massachusetts*

6	tablespoons butter, softened
1-1/2	cups sugar, *divided*
1	tablespoon grated lemon peel
2	eggs
2	egg whites
2-1/2	cups cake flour
2	tablespoons poppy seeds
1-1/2	teaspoons baking powder
1/2	teaspoon baking soda
1/2	teaspoon salt
1/4	teaspoon ground allspice
1-1/3	cups 1% buttermilk
1/4	cup lemon juice

In a large bowl, beat butter and 1-1/4 cups sugar until crumbly, about 2 minutes. Add lemon peel; mix well. Add eggs and egg whites, one at a time, beating well after each addition. Combine the flour, poppy seeds, baking powder, baking soda, salt and allspice. Gradually add to the butter mixture alternately with the buttermilk, beating well after each addition.

Transfer to a 10-in. tube pan heavily coated with cooking spray. Bake at 350° for 40-45 minutes or until a toothpick inserted near the center comes out clean. Cool in pan for 10 minutes. Carefully run a knife around the edge of pan and center tube to loosen. Remove to a wire rack.

Meanwhile, in a small saucepan, combine the lemon juice and remaining sugar. Cook and stir until mixture comes to a boil; cook and stir 1-2 minutes longer or until the sugar is dissolved. Using a fork, poke holes in the top of cake. Gradually pour hot syrup over cake. Cool completely. **YIELD: 2 DOZEN SLICES.**

NUTRITION FACTS: 2 slices equals 266 calories, 8 g fat (4 g saturated fat), 52 mg cholesterol, 318 mg sodium, 47 g carbohydrate, 1 g fiber, 5 g protein. **DIABETIC EXCHANGES:** 3 starch, 1 fat.

four-berry smoothies ⓁⒻ ⓁⓈ ⓂⓁ

This smoothie tastes even more scrumptious when I think of how much money I save by whipping up my own at home. Filled with fruit, it keeps me satisfied and full of energy all day long.
—*Krista Johnson, Crosslake, Minnesota*

1-1/2	cups fat-free milk
1/2	cup frozen blackberries
1/2	cup frozen blueberries
1/2	cup frozen unsweetened raspberries
1/2	cup frozen unsweetened strawberries
2	tablespoons lemonade concentrate
1	tablespoon sugar
1/2	teaspoon vanilla extract

In a blender, combine all the ingredients. Cover and process until smooth. Pour into chilled glasses; serve immediately. **YIELD: 2 SERVINGS.**

NUTRITION FACTS: 1-1/2 cups equals 172 calories, 1 g fat (0.55 g saturated fat), 4 mg cholesterol, 100 mg sodium, 36 g carbohydrate, 4 g fiber, 8 g protein. **DIABETIC EXCHANGES:** 1-1/2 fruit, 1 fat-free milk.

four-berry smoothies

chocolate marvel cake

chocolate marvel cake ML

This chocolaty cake with its light and fluffy mocha frosting is deliciously moist. Fat-free milk and egg whites add protein while prunes add a dash of fiber for good measure.
—Pearl Watts, Cincinnati, Ohio

- 2 packages (5 ounces *each*) prune baby food
- 1 cup strong brewed coffee
- 1 cup fat-free milk
- 4 egg whites
- 2 teaspoons vanilla extract
- 2 cups all-purpose flour
- 2 cups sugar
- 3/4 cup baking cocoa
- 2 teaspoons baking soda
- 1 teaspoon baking powder
- 1/4 teaspoon salt

FROSTING:

- 6 tablespoons butter, softened
- 2-2/3 cups confectioners' sugar
- 1/4 cup baking cocoa
- 2 tablespoons fat-free milk
- 2 tablespoons strong brewed coffee
- 1 teaspoon vanilla extract

In a large bowl, combine 3 containers baby food, coffee, milk, egg whites and vanilla; beat until well blended. (Save remaining container of baby food for another use.) Combine the flour, sugar, cocoa, baking soda, baking powder and salt; add to coffee mixture. Beat for 2 minutes or until well blended (batter will be thin).

Pour into two 9-in. round baking pans that have been coated with cooking spray and lightly floured. Bake at 350° for 30-35 minutes or until cake pulls away from sides of pan. Cool for 10 minutes; remove from pans to wire racks to cool completely.

For frosting, in a small bowl, cream the butter, sugar and cocoa. Gradually add the milk, coffee and vanilla; beating well. Frost between layers and over top and sides of cake. **YIELD: 16 SERVINGS.**

NUTRITION FACTS: 1 slice equals 306 calories, 5 g fat (0 saturated fat), trace cholesterol, 614 mg sodium, 64 g carbohydrate, 0 fiber, 4 g protein. **DIABETIC EXCHANGES:** 3 starch, 1 fruit, 1 fat.

strawberry pie ML

There's plenty of sweet berry flavor in this refreshing dessert. Made with sugar-free gelatin and a graham cracker crust, this summery pie is easy to fix and attractive enough to serve to guests. I sometimes substitute fresh peaches and peach gelatin.
—D. Smith, Featerville-Trevose, Pennsylvania

- 2 pints fresh strawberries, hulled
- 2 tablespoons cornstarch
- 1-1/2 cups cold water
- 1 package (.3 ounce) sugar-free strawberry gelatin
- 3 tablespoons sugar
- 1 reduced-fat graham cracker crust (8 inches)
- 2 cups reduced-fat whipped topping

Set aside four whole berries for garnish. Slice remaining strawberries and set aside. In a large saucepan, combine cornstarch and water until smooth. Bring to a boil; cook and stir for 2 minutes or until thickened.

Remove from the heat; stir in gelatin and sugar until dissolved. Stir in sliced strawberries. Pour into the crust. Cover and refrigerate for 2 hours or until firm.

Cut reserved strawberries in half. Garnish each serving with whipped topping and a berry half. **YIELD: 8 SERVINGS.**

NUTRITION FACTS: 1 piece with 1/4 cup whipped topping equals 197 calories, 5 g fat (3 g saturated fat), trace cholesterol, 125 mg sodium, 33 g carbohydrate, 2 g fiber, 2 g protein. **DIABETIC EXCHANGES:** 1 starch, 1 fruit, 1 fat.

strawberry pie

raspberry smoothies

1 carton (8 ounces) frozen reduced-fat whipped topping, thawed, *divided*
1-1/2 cups cold fat-free milk
1 package (1/4 ounces) instant sugar-free chocolate pudding mix

In a small bowl, cut butter into flour until crumbly. Press into an 11-in. x 7-in. baking dish coated with cooking spray. Bake at 350° for 15-18 minutes or until lightly browned. Cool completely.

In a large bowl, beat cream cheese and sweetener until smooth. Fold in half of the whipped topping. Carefully spread over the crust.

In another large bowl, combine milk and pudding mix. Beat on low speed for 2 minutes. Let stand for 2 minutes or until soft-set. Spread over the cream cheese. Top with remaining whipped topping. YIELD: 15 SERVINGS.

NUTRITION FACTS: 1 serving equals 134 calories, 6 g fat, 6 mg cholesterol, 184 mg sodium, 14 g carbohydrate, 4 g protein. DIABETIC EXCHANGES: 1-1/2 fat, 1 starch.

raspberry smoothies ㋀ ㋜ ㋔

This simple smoothie is a nutritious choice for anyone on the go. Raspberries and banana give the not-too-sweet sipper its pleasant flavor.
—Heather Mate, Pitt Meadows, British Columbia

1 cup milk
1 cup fresh *or* frozen unsweetened raspberries
1 small ripe banana, cut into chunks
1/2 cup apple juice
1/2 cup raspberry yogurt

In a blender, combine all ingredients; cover and process until blended. Pour into chilled glasses; serve immediately. YIELD: 3 SERVINGS.

NUTRITION FACTS: 1 cup (prepared with 1% milk and reduced-fat yogurt) equals 147 calories, 2 g fat (1 g saturated fat), 8 mg cholesterol, 70 mg sodium, 29 g carbohydrate, 4 g fiber, 5 g protein. DIABETIC EXCHANGES: 1 fruit, 1 reduced-fat milk.

hot fudge sundae cake ㋜ ㋔

This fudgy cake is pure pleasure. It's a snap to make in the microwave, so it's great for busy weeknights.
—Florence Beer, Houlton, Wisconsin

1 cup all-purpose flour
3/4 cup sugar
2 tablespoons plus 1/4 cup baking cocoa, *divided*
2 teaspoons baking powder
1/4 teaspoon salt
1/2 cup fat-free milk
2 tablespoons canola oil
1 teaspoon vanilla extract
1/2 cup chopped pecans
1 cup packed brown sugar
1-3/4 cups boiling water
10 tablespoons reduced-fat whipped topping

In an ungreased 2-1/2-qt. microwave-safe dish, combine the flour, sugar, 2 tablespoons cocoa, baking powder and salt. Stir in milk, oil and vanilla until combined. Fold in nuts. Combine brown sugar and remaining cocoa; sprinkle over batter.

Pour boiling water over batter (do not stir). Microwave, uncovered, on high for 7-8 minutes or until top of cake springs back when lightly touched. Serve with whipped topping. YIELD: 10 SERVINGS.

NUTRITION FACTS: 1 piece equals 274 calories, 8 g fat (1 g saturated fat), trace cholesterol, 121 mg sodium, 50 g carbohydrate, 2 g fiber, 3 g protein. DIABETIC EXCHANGES: 2-1/2 starch, 1-1/2 fat.

Editor's Note: This recipe was tested in a 1,100-watt microwave.

chocolate cream dessert ㋛ ㋔

Our daughter and her boyfriend are both on restricted diets, so they appreciate having this yummy treat for birthdays and other gatherings. We all enjoy it, too!
—Ronald Scorse, Snowflake, Arizona

1/4 cup cold butter, cubed
1 cup all-purpose flour
1 package (8 ounces) reduced-fat cream cheese, softened
Artificial sweetener equivalent to 2 tablespoons sugar

light tiramisu

light tiramisu Ⓜ

I call this my "skinny" dessert. It tastes just like the traditional Italian dessert, but uses low-fat and sugar-free ingredients.
—*Jackie Newell, Roanoke, Virginia*

- 1 prepared angel food cake (8 inches), cut into 1-inch cubes
- 1/2 cup instant sugar-free cappuccino mix, *divided*
- 2 cups cold fat-free milk, *divided*
- 1 package (8 ounces) fat-free cream cheese, softened
- 1 package (1 ounce) sugar-free instant vanilla pudding mix
- 2 cups reduced-fat whipped topping
- 1/2 teaspoon baking cocoa

Place cake cubes in an ungreased 13-in. x 9-in. dish. In a small bowl, combine 1/4 cup cappuccino mix and 1/2 cup milk until dissolved. Pour over cake.

In a large bowl, beat cream cheese until fluffy. In another large bowl, combine the pudding mix, remaining cappuccino mix and milk; whisk until smooth and thickened.

Beat into the cream cheese and mix well. Fold in whipped topping; spoon over cake mixture. Refrigerate for 3 hours or overnight. Sprinkle the tiramisu with baking cocoa just before serving. **YIELD: 8 SERVINGS.**

NUTRITION FACTS: 1 serving equals 351 calories, 6 g fat (0 saturated fat), 3 mg cholesterol, 797 mg sodium, 62 g carbohydrate, trace fiber, 11 g protein. **DIABETIC EXCHANGES:** 4 starch, 1 fat.

lemon orange refresher Ⓛ Ⓛ Ⓜ

The tangy flavor of lemon and orange comes through sip after sip in this frosty drink. Not only is it cool and thirst-quenching, it's filled with calcium and vitamin C, too.
—*Jodi Tuell, Raymond, California*

- 1 cup fat-free milk
- 1 carton (6 ounces) reduced-fat lemon yogurt
- 1 can (6 ounces) frozen unsweetened orange juice concentrate
- 1 tablespoon honey
- 1 teaspoon vanilla extract
- 1/4 teaspoon orange extract
- 15 ice cubes
- 5 long strips orange *or* lemon peel, twisted into spirals

In a blender, combine the first seven ingredients; cover and process until slushy. Pour beverage into chilled glasses. Garnish with orange or lemon spirals. Serve immediately. **YIELD: 5 SERVINGS.**

NUTRITION FACTS: 1 cup equals 124 calories, 1 g fat (0.55 g saturated fat), 3 mg cholesterol, 57 mg sodium, 25 g carbohydrate, 0.55 g fiber, 5 g protein. **DIABETIC EXCHANGES:** 1-1/2 fruit, 1/2 fat-free milk.

lemon orange refresher

general index

This index lists every recipe by food category and/or major ingredient, so you can easily locate recipes to suit your needs.

alphabetical index

This index lists every recipe in alphabetical order so you can easily find your favorite recipes.